A Road Map to Creating Wealth: My Story

A Simple Book for Non-Financially Literate People

Sadiq Al Mulla

Copyright © 2023 Sadiq Al Mulla

All Rights Reserved

All rights reserved. No part of this book may be reproduced, stored in a retrieval system, or transmitted by any means, electronic, mechanical, photocopying, recording, or otherwise be copied for public or private use (other than for "fair use" as brief quotations embodied in articles and reviews) without prior written permission from the copyright holder.

Dedication

To my late father…

I often accompanied him on his travels and have been close to him since my childhood.

I learned from his experience, wisdom, and vision. He inspired me, trusted me, believed in me, and taught me how to grow up wisely.

To my late mother…

Who dedicated her life to taking care of me from childhood and supported me with a tremendous amount of love and care.

About the Author

Sadiq Almulla is a renowned expert in the fields of Finance, Management, Investment, and Banking, with an illustrious career spanning over thirty years. Throughout his journey in the financial and banking world, he has held leadership and management roles in both the private and public sectors, amassing a wealth of experience and knowledge that has made him a prominent name in the Finance and Banking Industry.

As a performance-driven professional, Sadiq has achieved remarkable success in leading and managing businesses. He is known for his expertise in "build, operate, and transfer" and "fix, operate, and transfer" business strategies, which have contributed to his reputation as a seasoned financial and management expert.

Over the course of his career, Sadiq has been involved in various diversified business ventures in the private and public sectors. Drawing upon his extensive expertise, he has created wealth and financial success, enriching the content of his book with practical value.

Having gained invaluable experience and achieved significant wealth through his journey, Sadiq decided to share his success story in order to benefit and inspire others. From his humble beginnings as a Trainee Officer, he steadily climbed the ranks to hold a top regional management post, overseeing operations in the Middle East and North Africa for one of the largest international financial institutions, HSBC BANK MIDDLE EAST.

Sadiq's influence extended beyond his corporate roles, as he actively participated in several boards and committees, including serving on the Board of Directors for HSBC Middle East Finance Company in the UAE and HSBC Global Processing Centre in Cairo, Egypt. He was also a prominent member of the Executive Committee for Bankers Business Group in the UAE and chaired the Advisory Committee for Dubai Modern Educational School for two years. Sadiq also served as the Chief Administration and Finance Officer for Zayed University for seven years, with remarkable achievements.

Educationally accomplished, Sadiq holds a master's degree from the University of Bournemouth, England, and a Master of Quality Management from the University of Wollongong, Australia. His expertise has been recognized internationally, leading to frequent nominations for prestigious conferences and training sessions at renowned institutes such as IMD (Institute of Management Development) in Lausanne, Switzerland, London Business School, Oxford University in the United Kingdom, and University of Duke in the United States. Furthermore, he has shared his insights as a speaker, moderator, and panelist in various business-related events for private and public institutions.

Presently, Sadiq Almulla serves as an independent Advisor and Investor in the Stock Market and Real Estate, leveraging his vast experience and acumen to navigate these dynamic markets.

Through his book, "A Road Map to Creating Wealth: My Story," Sadiq Almulla aims to inspire and guide non-financially literate individuals on their own journey to financial success, offering practical insights and valuable lessons from his remarkable career and accomplishments.

Contents

Prologue 1

Introduction 12

Chapter 1: Financial Literacy 21

Chapter 2: The Psychology of Money 48

Chapter 3: Saving 63

Chapter 4: Budgeting 76

Chapter 5: Debts 91

Chapter 6: Compound Interest / Profit 107

Chapter 7: Investing 123

Chapter 8: Investing in ETFs, Mutual Funds, and Bonds 140

Chapter 9: Entrepreneurship 154

Chapter 10: Currency and Commodities Trading 168

Chapter 11: Investment in Real Estate 181

Chapter 12: Diversifying Your Investment Portfolio 195

Chapter 13: The Success Story of Sadiq Al Mulla 210

<u>Prologue</u>

"Inside every self-made man is a poor kid who followed his dream."

-Anonymous

In a world influenced by social media personalities, you might have read a little, if not a lot, about self-made millionaires. Or maybe somewhere you heard people talking about self-made personalities and their success stories, taking them as an inspiration. But have you ever wondered how all these self-made people reached where they are today? In no way can anyone claim that life allowed them to have an easy pass or, for some reason, life became extra sweet to them as it might appear from the surface level. Then, what is so different about the journey that sets them apart from the rest of the world?

Let me give you a little insight into the secret of a self-made man. Similar to any other person, a self-made person leads an ordinary life, and at times, they go through a vale of tears for eternity, yet this never stops them from dreaming. Even when the world tells them how far-fetched their goals are, they refuse to lose hope during the most unkind days. In short, a self-made man is someone who believes he can achieve anything and never lets anything weigh him down. His strong mentality allows him to stand tall against all the odds, while he refuses to stay in one place just because that provides him with the comfort of his home.

How do I know all this so accurately? Well, it is because this is about me drawing from my very own experiences of becoming a worthy self-made man, and I own every aspect of it with all the credibility. That is the core reason why a person like me, who has always worked day and night to achieve a successful lifestyle, would never shy away from openly sharing any part of their success story. I am proud of this amazing journey, and I want more people to realize that if I can achieve all this by developing certain disciplines, then why can't they? Yes, there is no hard and fast way to get success. It is not an overnight process, but trust me, a systematic plan can make all their dreams come true.

Initially, it is nerve-wracking to find a correct strategy, especially when you are new to this field. In such a case, having a mentor would be great, but is it really possible to find someone who would prevent you from hitting a dead end?

Well, on such an occasion, I, as a financial expert, am always open to helping anyone who would want to be mentored by me. All you need to do is reach me through my email address, and together, we will pave the road toward your goal.

To my surprise, many people prefer not to talk about the

strategies they have developed because, firstly, they feel this will give an easy way out to the newcomers. Secondly, some people fear that their wealth might be taken away from them if they ever share their secrets with anyone. But, I don't see the point in gate-keeping any of the solutions I have developed so far; instead, I want people to learn valuable lessons from my experiences and thrive in their lives. Taking all these aspects into consideration, I finally decided to develop this roadmap that will act as a mentor on its own and will aid you in getting rid of any stumbling blocks in your career.

I was born into a family that owned a small business. At first, it feels like a great deal to be born into a family that has a history of trade. However, little do people know that my father had a troubled childhood. He lost his father at the age of 15. This dates back to the early 1940s when UAE was nothing like it is today. During those days, this city was nothing more than a deserted land where my father and his siblings struggled every day to survive. My father did not get a chance to attend any formal mode of education since it wasn't an option in Dubai; however, with his intellect, he still managed to learn basic reading and writing skills, learned a little math, and, at the same time started a business on his own.

Certainly, he did not get a chance to study in his childhood like other merchants around him, particularly those merchants who came from India in the early 50s and 60s. Nonetheless, my father had the vision to lead the market, so he mustered the courage to start something he could call his own and succeeded. He was no diploma holder. In fact, he had no formal education. However, he knew how to trade through his immense experience and trust me, it was no less than a blessing that we, as his children, were bestowed by his wisdom.

Maybe it was because of my father that I, along with my brothers, learned the art of trading at a very young age. During our school life, I still remember we used to work with our father after we got done with classes or during our summer vacations. At that time, I thought trading was always fun, but now, when I look back, I think I found trading fun because I was doing it with my father. He taught me everything slowly and gradually, one step at a time. Even though his tactics were outdated and his strategies were not very well-planned, I still believe it was he who laid the foundation for my plans.

I often wonder, what if my father did not show us the road to trading? What could have happened then? On a serious note, neither do I have an answer to that question, nor can I even bear to think otherwise.

Trading was not something that I did half-heartedly or because I was required to earn money. Instead, it was something that I loved doing, and I wholeheartedly put my soul into it. This is the field that has changed me as a person and turned me into what I am today.

During the early years of my life, my affection for trading piqued so much that I willingly opted for a degree in the field of business administration. People would think that a degree might not be that helpful in learning the trade, but I have seen my father struggling without a degree. Yes, he did establish a business on his own merit, but his struggles were real, and I, being the witness to his struggle, can never turn a blind eye to the fact that a degree and formal education can make a lot of difference.

So, at this point, where I had some first-hand experience, I planned to set up my game through books this time. I knew getting a bachelor's degree in business administration would not open the doors of opportunities for me because, believe it or not, trading does require commitment and patience, and I had to master those too to get the best idea of the trading world, and so I did. I made the degree my goal at first, and when I achieved my initial goal, I moved to the next one. Not for a second did I consider taking a break because I knew the world was changing rapidly. And when the world is not taking a pause, then why should I be at a halt? Certainly, that would leave me behind in the race. This was my motivation that kept me running day and night without looking back or without stopping. In my vision, it was just me and solely me who was a part of this race, and I had to win this challenge, come what may.

I believe it was the year 1983 when I graduated and finally got my degree in business. I still feel that it was one of the biggest achievements of my life that made me the happiest, and why would it not? I had finally taken the first step in the direction of realizing my long-cherished dream of becoming a successful man, someone who was not dependent on anyone. And now, the time to finally become the self-sufficient adult I always dreamt of was here. I was halfway there, and from that standpoint, I felt like I could achieve everything I wanted to.

However, I soon realized that the real test of life was waiting for me outside of the premises of the university. I realized I was standing at a phase where I needed to make a rational decision to align my theoretical knowledge with my skills in such a way that it gave me the maximum benefits. Trust me when I say it was not at all easy for me to become the very version of an adult that I aspired to be since a young age.

In search of becoming an independent adult, I started working at a financial institution. Indeed, this was a major challenge in my life where I had to apply what I had learned so far while mastering a lot more complex strategies that my father never got a chance to learn. Though this phase of my life was a little rough because I was on my own, it was the beginning of my journey, and it felt like a surreal dream.

At first, it was exhausting since I could not rely on my father anymore, and practically, I was still a beginner, so I did what every beginner should do. I started building my experience from scratch and chose to dive into the financial world with my little knowledge of the real world. But who could have thought that my little to no knowledge of the financial world would allow me to see a morning like this where I can think about investing money and further develop my plans to continue living my lifelong dream?

However, even when I felt like everything was going according to plan, I did not dare to become complacent. Instead, I started doing my research on the most effective ways through which investments can be made. I never believed in complex or easy-to-achieve plans, so I developed a plan of my own that was fool-proof, one that would do exactly what it was designed to do. Meanwhile, I worked day and night to develop a strategic plan to make my dream come true without feeling demotivated by any of my competitors. In all honesty, I never felt affected by anyone around me. I do not know how most people would perceive it, but for me, minding my own business was my power. This is what allowed me to stay focused on one path, undeterred, and this is what stopped me from having the urge to deviate. The only thing that mattered to me was my dream, and I had to achieve it at any cost. The dream that I once saw became my inspiration, and it became my only motive to move forward. Even on the darkest day when I felt like leaving everything behind, it was the same dream that gave me courage. From day to night, I worked hard to enhance my knowledge, polish my skills, and become a better version of myself because that was the only way to achieve the goals that were ostensibly too high for me.

Finally, I got to see the day when I got my first promotion, and since then, I have kept going like nothing was holding me back. Within the span of six years, I was frequently promoted from trainee officer in a local bank to main branch manager. I don't have the words to explain how I felt during those times. I was over the moon. I had no one to be thankful for but me. My hard work was finally paying off. With every passing day, I was stepping closer to the dream I had carved all my life, but this was not the end. Soon, I got a chance to switch from a small, local financial institution to one of the leading international banks. This was a superb opportunity for someone like me who has always thrived for growth, and so I took the opportunity in a heartbeat. I started as an executive bank manager while pursuing a master's degree in business administration.

I started from the bottom, but with relentless perseverance and dedication, I got a chance to climb the ladder of success all the way from a trainee officer to the middle management level and then finally to the top senior management level. At this point, I had everything that I desired, yet I still felt the hunger to go on and achieve what once seemed an implausible goal—to multiply money and accumulate wealth. All I wanted was a chance to lunge forward and make the next move in my career. It wasn't until 2012 that I decided to leave my job. The economy had fully recovered from the global financial meltdown of 2008, and it seemed like a perfect time to establish a real estate business. It was worth giving a shot since the real estate market was booming every passing day. I started taking some specialized courses on the side to strengthen my knowledge of the real estate world while working on my investment plan.

Everything was going smoothly. I established my own firm and managed to secure the investment within the span of a year. Right then, a new opportunity knocked on my door. To my surprise, I got an offer from the government sector of the UAE. Here, one thing was clear: opportunities like this do not approach you often, so I grabbed it without giving it another thought, but this does not mean that I had to leave what I started. I stayed focused and continued managing my real estate investments, even on weekends, while also keeping a formal government job.

After gaining experience, getting good exposure, and saving enough money, it was time for me to start focusing on my investment plan and begin reaping lucrative profits. At this point, I made yet another audacious career move by quitting my job. This decision was mostly made so that I could spend more time with my family and pursue my passion—investments. However, the year 2020 didn't go as planned, and before I could quit my job, I lost my father in May 2020. We were still coping with the loss when my mother passed away in August 2020. The sudden shock was a turning point for me, and it made me quit my job on three months' notice. In December 2020, I finally said goodbye to my career as a senior government employee.

Without adding any element of exaggeration, it was a lot more challenging than all of my previous jobs. It was a road full of bumps for me. At first, a formal stock market was not available in the UAE, and stock trade had to be done through direct contacts from the sellers or through the share department of the company, where the sellers inform the company of their intention to sell the shares if any is interested in buying. The shares department was in no way any better since they used to decide stock prices entirely based on the last traded share price, which was limited to only a few transactions a month.

This practice continued till a few brokerage companies, acting as a broker between buyers and sellers in the absence of formal stock markets, came into existence. Soon, the stock market in the UAE was established, making it a lot more convenient to trade. But for me, trading started long ago, even when the stock market did not exist in the UAE. I chose to trade at an early stage because deep down, I knew that in the not-so-distant future, trading stocks would be all the rage in the UAE.

As a starter, I invested in UK and USA stock markets to gain experience and diversify my small portfolio investment. That's how I built my portfolio, which expanded with the establishment of the UAE stock exchange.

The journey to my growth and success was challenging as I took some risky, bumpy roads to reach where I am today. At times, it cost me a lot of trouble and loss of opportunities. Why? Because I always chose to abide by laws and play a fair game. Ethics, discipline, honesty, humanity, morality, and spirituality governed my growth and success.

I'm glad I trusted my intuition and went with my guts to achieve what I have today. Now, when I look back, I can tell it was worth the go.

"Winners are not born; they are self-made."

-Pat Summitt

Introduction

Throughout your corporate career, have you ever felt so disheartened and undervalued from the job that you wanted to resign on an immediate basis but could not because you did not have any financial security? Well, this is how the corporate world runs. You work day and night but to no avail. Your work is back-breaking, but you still live from paycheck to paycheck, and in all honesty, you will forever continue doing so unless you strengthen your game and familiarize yourself with the world of investment and stocks.

Initially, it does appear daunting, especially when you have little to no financial knowledge, but once you eliminate the fear of losing, you will witness the gateway connecting you to the world of riches.

However, one thing should be made clear here: choosing a path other than a 9 to 5 job does not mean you get to slack or live an easy life from day one. Instead, it is quite the contrary. This is where life throws the worst challenges at you the most. Since it is a less traveled road, you will most likely find yourself alone. This feeling can sometimes weigh you down, especially when you cannot find any credible sources where you can look up the solution to your problems.

This is exactly when you should start studying the market trends and familiarize yourself with the work of successful people from the same field who were once as clueless as you. Learn to follow their roadmaps and strategies until you develop your own, but do not forget that sticking too long to one strategy does not necessarily mean consistency; sometimes, it can show contrasting effects.

This being said, gaining wealth is not always about strategies. Instead, it has much to do with being a potential risk-taker, and there are no two ways to it. If you are not a risk-taker, you can never put the odds of success in your favor. Believe me or not, this is the story of every wealthy person you will ever encounter in your life. They will always have a back story where they took the risk despite not being too sure and still managed to turn the odds in their favor.

However, this does not imply that you should not assess the risk involved in something not working in your favor. In no way should blind risk-taking be promoted; this is not a round of gambling. Bear in mind not every risk is worth taking, and you should never blindly hop on the first opportunity you get. Instead, try asking yourself, "Will this bring me closer to my goal before taking any risk?"

This is where this book comes in handy, or to be precise, the financial roadmap that is specifically developed to make your journey a lot easier and less bumpy.

People who have never been remotely close to finance and management would find it a lot easier to go through this book without worrying about all those technicalities. This is a guide where you can find everything ranging from my personal experience to tried and tested ways through which a successful investment can be made possible.

You might want to approach this book with certain presuppositions, like if it is a finance book, it will certainly be boring, and I think, at this point, it is safe to have the benefit of the doubt. But, here is a thing. I, myself have been directed to countless books in my life, so I know how it feels like to read a boring book just to lose all of the remaining motivation.

Every chapter of this book is designed in a way that will cater to almost all of the presumed effects from all angles, making sure to eliminate the unwanted jargon for the convenience of the readers. By the end of this book, you will develop a rather reliable skillset in money management, and you will be surprised to see how much your knowledge of investing, finances, and budgeting has expanded.

This self-explanatory book is designed for people who struggle to manage their finances independently. It will show them a road map to creating wealth.

Chapter 1 begins with the importance of financial literacy among people so they may make informed financial decisions. The chapter intends to highlight the fact that people don't pay as much attention to saving and investment as they do to spending. That's because they don't have a plan. And they don't have one because they are not financially literate. They lack knowledge that can make them wealthy. At first, this could be seen as people's lack of interest in developing an investment plan; however, this is not always the case with everyone. There could be other factors that might have affected their experience with the idea of finance management.

The chapter stresses the importance of gaining financial wisdom. It precisely talks about the need for schools to develop financial literacy in students. No proper awareness of personal finances results in the failure of financial literacy and projects the image that if it is not a part of the Standard Assessment Tests (SATs), it is not important enough to learn.

Chapter 2 builds upon the idea of commission, budgeting, opportunity costs, and so on. This chapter is specially designed, keeping the needs of the younger generation in mind. They are the ones who need to understand the importance of budgeting at the right time. This is a valuable lesson that should be learned at an early age. Since they always have a place where they want to spend money, they should be taught how to invest money rather than just spend it. The psychology of money advocates the idea of instilling the worth of money at a young age. The earlier, the better.

Chapter 3 takes the readers a step ahead in their journey with the help of a little guide to saving money because where achieving financial stability is about investment, it is equally important to have a track of where it is being spent. I'll go ahead and drop a hint here: Beware of credit cards!

So far, I have realized that people do not hesitate to save money because they failed miserably the first time they tried. Instead, most of the time, it is because they prefer to rely more on the baseless myths that they picked from somewhere. None can tell the origin of these myths, but you can tell these myths were spread intentionally to maintain class differences. In this chapter, the widely believed myths attached to saving money are discussed to promote saving on an individual level.

Budgeting is the most critical part of the process, and if you think you can be a part of riches by just saving a teeny-tiny amount, then I am sorry to burst your bubble; your approach is entirely wrong. Budgeting is the order that would never let your house collapse if done correctly and persistently.

Chapter 4 strongly captures the ample ways through which budgeting can be done easily and sufficiently while eradicating the complex procedures that nobody would want to learn.

Chapter 5 is dedicated to the role of debts in modern-day life. This chapter discusses the nature of debts. The good loans and bad loans. The types of loans people can take out and the ones they should refrain from. Although relying on loans is something to be wary of, there are a few types of loans you can opt for when needed. For instance, personal loans, mortgage loans, or car loans. On the other hand, the chapter will also discuss the adverse effects of a few debts on your financial status. For example, credit card debts.

The chapter will discuss how credit card debt is detrimental to your financial growth and what you can do to cultivate healthy spending habits to avoid accumulating this kind of debt.

As you delve into a more efficient way to save money, you will be introduced to *Chapter 6.* Here, the compound interest/profit and its understanding will provide insight into how to plan your future accordingly. This might look slightly overwhelming, but as you read on, it will get easier for you. Besides that, this chapter will provide a simple, step-by-step guide on how to make compound interest/profit work in your best interest.

Chapter 7 is a detailed lesson on investing in stocks. The mechanics of buying, selling, and owning stocks are discussed at length here. Furthermore, the processes of stock exchanges, the price fluctuation of stocks, and the ideal time to buy and sell stocks will be explained to the readers. They will also be introduced to active and passive approaches to investing in stocks, dividends, and the types of stocks.

When you embark on the journey of investing, you better not get on board without setting investment goals. Your goals serve as a barometer to measure your performance against time. What are investment goals? How do you go about short-term and long-term investments? What are their merits and demerits? This and much more is what you will get to learn in this very crucial chapter that advocates the multiple ways to minimize investment risk and maximize profits.

Chapter 8 will shed light on the correct placement of assets through which investment could be doubled and secured. With that, this chapter will go into the depth of investing in Bonds, Mutual Funds, Exchange Traded Funds, and will further describe their merits.

Moving onto *Chapter 9,* which emphasizes the significance of entrepreneurship and the wonders it is capable of doing. Since people find entrepreneurship risky, they usually ignore its countless benefits. Yet this is the one thing that can change a person's circumstances in a very short span.

If you want to learn the power of entrepreneurship, then this chapter is for you. Follow this step-by-step guide on how to become an entrepreneur and take a leap toward your goal.

Chapter 10 begins with a short idea on how trading can be done right, which later draws upon the concept of Forex trading and investment that could be made through commodities and valuable metals. With that, this chapter also explores the concepts surrounding options trading and discusses its pros, cons, and some of the worth-mentioning tips.

Chapter 11 progresses with profitable acquisitions and their management, usually achieved through the investment done with the help of real estate. Real estate is indeed profitable, but the determining factor is how one should start dabbling in this type of investment. This chapter addresses the said conundrum and further elaborates on the advantages of real estate investment and why it should be your next big move.

Chapter 12 is among the most critical chapters. It will cater to the types of risks involved in investment and how you can deal with them by virtue of a rather novel concept known as diversification. Through diversification, you can mitigate the risk around your assets. This chapter highlights the idea of diversifying your investment through multiple exposures rather than limiting it to one source. It is a must-read for people who are new to this game but, at the same time, they want to play safe.

Chapter 13 handles the life story of a man who climbed the ladder of financial status on his own. That man is me. The final chapter incorporates the struggles and challenges that I had to go through to achieve where I am right now. It is my dream to see more and more people achieving great wealth without having to go through the hindrances that held me back. I believe you can begin a successful financial journey and thrive at any age if you have the correct strategy. And so I will share my proven strategy and roadmap to wealth with the readers. I will encapsulate all relevant lessons pertaining to how I overcame the economic cycles, dealt with the ups and downs of growth and recession over the course of 35 years, and achieved one milestone after another. I will walk you through how I made my first USD 1 million, then USD 5 million, and then continued to over USD 20 million!

Remember, *A Road Map to Creating Wealth* is not just a book but a legit roadmap, a strategic plan that desires to guide not-so-financially-literate people to the path of accumulating wealth. So, without further ado, let's begin…

"Finance without a strategy is just numbers, and strategy without finance is dreaming."

-Emmanuel Faber

Chapter 1: Financial Literacy

"If you don't find a way to make money while you sleep, you will work until you die."

-Warren Buffett

There are thousands and thousands of ways to earn money, but the real concern is how many of us are aware of these distinctive approaches. Forget the tricky part; most of us do not even possess the basic skillset required to manage our finances efficiently.

As per a recent study, most well-developed countries fall into the ratio of 31% to 51% concerning financial literacy, and when it comes to underdeveloped countries, they can barely make up 15% of the ratio. That being said, in the contemporary world, one in every three adults is financially literate, making 33% of adults financially illiterate around the globe. Apparently, for some people, this seems like an inconsequential idea. Others might not even consider it a thing. It is not their fault. They were never taught the importance of financial literacy.

Throughout their lives, they were never made to learn the basics of finance management. Naturally, they would not understand its importance, making them vulnerable to multiple pitfalls. And once they fall into it, they cannot tell how to break free themselves. This explains why almost half of this generation has bad credit. They casually take out a loan or get things on credit just because it enchants them, but what they forget to calculate is the fact that this enchantment lasts for a brief moment, leaving them indebted for a long period.

And you know what is surprising? People fail to understand that the excessive use of credit cards will never help them secure a better future. If you look closely, this is not a very accurate strategy to improve living standards; instead, it could certainly be efficient if you desire to lose the remaining finances. But to restore the long-lost finances by going into debt or taking out a loan is a big NO.

This is where the young generation needs to wake up from their luxurious dream and realize the horrendous intention of credit card companies. They do not aim to fulfill your dreams; instead, they are the termites built to creep into your savings and eat the very last of your hard-earned money. Thus, now is the time for the new generation to start taking their finances more seriously. If they do not learn the art of finance management at this point, they will forever be stuck in the vicious cycle of financial instability.

It is high time for people to start learning the significance of financial literacy before it's too late and before they get completely submerged in this mire of debt. Because no matter how reckless a person is, they still would not want to pass the debt as a generational gift to the upcoming generations. That is why getting a grip on your savings while learning the basics of financial literacy is important.

Let's suppose you start learning about financial literacy at this instant; who knows, you might be able to pass generational wealth to the young kids instead of loads of generational debt. Believe me, this is not just a far-fetched idea; it can happen to anyone, and I am a living example. All you need to do is dive into the world of financial literacy, and you will be able to understand ample novel ways to save your money as well as double your income. What could be better than that?

New Generation and Financial Literacy

First thing first, why is it of utmost importance for the young generation to be familiar with financial literacy?

Apparently, the younger generation is tech-savvy and a know-it-all. They do not believe in asking for help from anyone, nor do they believe in discussing anything with the experts around them. Certainly, they think they are the jack of all trades, but being the master of none can have some serious implications. This is precisely the case with youngsters, who are more likely to fall into financial traps. They are already a young, optimistic generation who lives by the motto of YOLO (You Only Live Once). Their reckless behavior toward money is highly dangerous, and they will most likely become victims of financial scams.

This is not only due to their careless attitude or lavish spending style; they are equally unaware of how they can improve their living standards. They are clueless about the risk approaching them owing to their little to no financial literacy.

So far, people have alienated this whole idea of financial literacy, which is why it is essential to bring up this topic at a rather early age instead of treating it in a vacuum. They should learn to be able to make informed decisions while managing their finances on their own.

But at what age should one start teaching financial literacy?

The answer should be simple. At what age do parents want their children to start following proper etiquette? A kid unknowingly starts picking up the basic mannerism at an early age. So why cannot they start learning about their finances at the same age? After all, their future is at stake. They should be very much conscious while making this decision. After all, not being exposed to financial literacy at the right time will seriously affect their children's lives.

Through financial literacy, young adults learn to start saving money early while also realizing the value of budgeting. Moreover, with finances and budgeting, they get an idea of the things that are worth buying and the things that only add to the expenses.

As per some of the studies, most of the schools show strict resistance toward the idea of providing any real-world experiences to the students. They brush this topic under the rug, claiming these kids are too young to deal with such pressure. This means that when a student graduates, he is still not prepared enough to deal with basic finances on his own, so the question is, what kind of rote learning schools are providing at this age and date?

Another report conducted in the United States suggests that most young adults opt for the frequent use of credit cards because they do not possess enough knowledge to deal with their finances. As a result, they get trapped in the world of credit and debt to make ends meet.

However, more and more people are now seen to be inclined toward being financially literate. They are heavily voicing their concerns regarding the growth opportunities of future generations and show a strong urge to be familiarized with financial literacy. They believe that avoiding the taboo of money is not a solution; it is high time schools and formal institutions should make financial literacy mandatory.

Financial Education Should Be Mandatory

History is full of names of prominent personalities who went broke despite earning millions of dollars during the peak of their career.

Can you believe that Michael Jackson, the king of pop music, was forced to the brink of bankruptcy in 2007 when he was unable to pay back a $25 million loan? He was spending money as he would never run out until he finally did. At his death in 2009, he reportedly owed more than $300 million.

Another valid example is the former heavyweight champion Mike Tyson, who made more money in his time than any other boxer in history, nearly half a billion dollars. He was spending like there was no tomorrow, buying stuff like crazy and relishing his wild lifestyle. His spending routine led to his bankruptcy. In an interview in 2010, Tyson said, *"I am totally broke."*

It should be a real concern. How did this happen? How in the world can someone with millions of dollars go broke? Honestly, this a tough task, but without having basic financial literacy, the 'broke' status can be achieved in a blink. So many people make a great amount of money, but by the end of their careers, they get pushed to the limit of bankruptcy. This would have never happened if they had been taught how to manage their finances and were made aware of the significance of financial literacy.

It is human nature to want to spend money like there is no tomorrow. The masses absolutely despise going calculative, treating it as a burden. On the other hand, people with an obscene amount of money think there will never be an end to it, not knowing when this all will end. This concludes that having great assets and a good amount of money would never guarantee financial stability. People with high incomes can go broke, people with a stable amount of money in their bank account can go bankrupt, and nothing can prevent this from happening until and unless a person is financially literate enough to double the money.

Suppose a person was earning $100 initially. His family had to struggle to manage the expenses in that little amount. Later, he got a 40% appraisal, but his family was still struggling to make ends meet. Even though his income increased, their living conditions did not change for the better, and they continued to live a life of discomfort. This is because the family was not familiar with the idea of financial literacy.

Right after the appraisal, they started spending money on things that had no material worth. This would not have happened if the family had financial wisdom, where they would have chosen to invest the extra cash in something valuable instead of spending on useless stuff.

There is a common myth surrounding the idea of money management. People believe having good money management skills is about owning a filthy amount, whereas this is quite the contrary. Money management starts from a small amount, and slowly and gradually, this number grows to a larger amount.

"When money realizes that it is in good hands, it wants to stay and multiply in those hands."

-Idowu Koyenikan

With the internet boom and technology, this generation has opened uncountable doors to success. Nonetheless, they still fail to find reliable ways to invest their hard-earned money. Most of the younger generation is susceptible to financial traps. Their one wrong financial decision often pushes them to the brink of helplessness and, in some extreme cases, death.

There are so many things that people today are doing wrong when it comes to managing their finances. Let's take a look at what has worsened the financial condition of people around the world:

- They try to get rich the quickest way possible and end up wasting a lot of time and money. Know that getting rich slowly is fine.
- They take an uncalculated risk and incur losses in their investments. This, in turn, demotivates them.
- They don't educate themselves on money matters.
- They are not bold enough to act or make a financial decision when everyone is freaking out. Also, they are not cautious when everyone is toasting each other. They fail to believe that going opposite everyone else can be financially rewarding.
- They are impatient and don't invest slowly over time. They don't monitor their investments and leave them alone to mature.
- They are into using credit cards for convenience. The interest rate, when calculated, is huge. Thus, they accumulate a hefty amount of credit card debt.
- They don't enjoy the journey. Saving is good, but a balance is required when it comes to spending and saving. Most people either save, save, save…or spend, spend, spend.

Financial literacy is a serious matter and should not be neglected at any cost. As voiced above, financial education should be made mandatory, especially in schools and colleges. Though it should have been made a part of the curriculum long ago, it was observed that almost every school finds it uncomfortable to have a money-related conversation with their students. Even though this could be the scenario for certain schools, this cannot be considered an acceptable reason.

Schools are responsible for turning a kid into a responsible adult. Keeping this in mind, they should find effective strategies and approaches to help students in the long run. Thus, a school that focuses on financial education early on produces more responsible adults. When they enter the real world, these adults become a hundred times better at financing their assets than others.

This is why parents need to realize that introducing kids to financial literacy is essential so that:

- They can learn to differentiate between needs and wants. Training the children to think that everything they desire should not be purchased is important. Instead, they should learn to calculate the material value of every object to see if they are investing in it or wasting their money.
- The earlier they start saving, the more comfortable their life will become.
- A child with financial literacy will always be empowered.
- Since they know how to manage their finances efficiently, they will never have to worry about money.
- Well-equipped adults are the product of financial literacy. Always remember that illiteracy will breed ill-equipped adults.

To be exact, creating a generation with financial literacy is a must so that an adult does not feel liable for the mistakes his younger version once committed.

Financial Literacy and Its Benefits

A widely believed idea is that knowledge is power. It sounds cliché, but it could not be more accurate in this case. Having financial literacy allows one to have complete autonomy over one's money. The more a person is equipped with financial knowledge, the more empowered he will get. This is the key to living a happy, prosperous life without having to rely on anyone.

Here are some of the benefits that prove why financial literacy is of massive importance and why people should be paying this concept more attention:

1. Ability to Make Better Financial Decisions

Financial decisions are the foundation of a successful life. So, really, it's hard to go on living without making them! Decisions like selecting insurance, investments, loans, and a suitable credit card have an impact on your life. They have consequences. Having a reasonable amount of knowledge that enables you to make sound financial decisions can keep you from adverse consequences.

2. Effective Management of Money and Debt

Money management is key to keeping your finances in order. Creating and sticking to a budget will help you track your spending and make informed decisions about how much money you spend each month. This includes making sure you have a savings account as well as paying off debt—both of which are essential for your financial security.

3. Better Equipped to Reach Financial Goals

In today's world, being a financially literate person equips you to start or further your financial goals. By becoming more aware of your own finances and spending habits, you can make better decisions that lead to better financial lives. You can purchase a home, buy a car, and save for college! It means that you have the knowledge and skills to take control of your money and make smart decisions. You'll know what to do with it, where it goes, how much you need and when you need it.

4. Saving for Retirement and Emergencies

We all have different financial goals, but we all share a common desire to make our money work for us. Financial literacy helps you save for retirement and emergencies. It also helps you sleep better at night because no matter how much or little you have saved, you don't see yourself depending on someone else financially. To be able to manage your money well in a world where interest rates may rise or fall at any time is, believe me, something that reduces stress and anxiety a great deal.

5. Reducing Expenses and Investing

Financial literacy is the key to controlling expenses and making money. It helps you explore a multitude of investment options and teaches you how to manage them so you can make your own financial plan. Without having prior knowledge about investment options and their merits and demerits, there is always a risk of losing money and becoming demotivated in the process.

Must-Know Finance Terminologies

Have you ever thought about how rich people continue to make money? What do they do that is so different from what others do? The answer is surprisingly straightforward: they do their homework! They put in efforts to educate themselves on financial matters. They acquire financial knowledge so that they can use it to manage their money by spending it wisely and saving more.

Managing finances does not necessarily have to be a complex process, especially when dealing with the basics of finance management. Yet, people often feel instantly demotivated owing to the use of technical terminologies. Here are some of the widely used finance terms that will aid those who are starting their financial journey in understanding the many concepts of finance that they come across. Every person, regardless of his education and occupation, must be aware of these common terms:

1. Inflation

Inflation occurs when the market sees a sudden rise in prices while decreasing the purchasing power over a given period of time. In simpler terms, inflation is when a large amount of money starts chasing goods with little quantity. It is caused by three major factors.

Example: Imagine you go to the store with $10 to buy a pizza. Last year, the same pizza cost $8. However, when you arrive at the store, you find out that the price of the pizza has increased to $12. This increase in the price of the pizza is an example of inflation.

Inflation is the general increase in the prices of goods and services in an economy over time. It means that your money's purchasing power has decreased, as you now need more money to buy the same things you used to buy for less. This can be caused by various factors, such as increased production costs, higher demand for goods and services, changes in the supply of money, and more. Inflation is a common economic phenomenon that central banks and governments aim to manage to ensure stable economic conditions.

2. Interest/Profit Rate

Financial interest/profit refers to the money earned or paid for the use of borrowed money or the return earned on invested funds. Let's look at a simple example to understand this concept better:

Imagine you have $1,000 saved up, and you decide to lend it to a friend who wants to start a small business. You agree that they will pay you back the $1,000 in one year, along with an additional $100 as interest. In this case, the $100 is the financial interest you're earning on your loan.

On the flip side, let's say you decide to invest that same $1,000 in a savings account that offers an annual interest rate of 5%. After one year, your investment will have grown to $1,050. The $50 increase is the financial interest you've earned on your investment.

Financial interest can be earned through various types of financial instruments such as loans, bonds, savings accounts, certificates of deposit, and investments in stocks or mutual funds. It's the compensation you receive for allowing someone else to use your money temporarily or the reward for putting your money to work in an investment that generates returns over time.

3. Opportunity Cost

Opportunity cost refers to the value of the next best alternative that you forego when you make a decision to pursue one option over another. It represents the potential benefits or profits you could have gained from choosing a different option. Here's a brief example:

Let's say you have $10,000 to invest, and you're considering two options: Option A is to invest in Stock X, which historically has provided an average annual return of 8%. Option B is to invest in a Savings Account with a guaranteed annual interest rate of 2%.

If you choose Option A and invest in Stock X, after one year, your investment would grow by:

Investment Growth = Initial Investment * Rate of Return

Investment Growth = $10,000 * 0.08

Investment Growth = $800

If you choose Option B and invest in the Savings Account, after one year, your investment would grow by:

Investment Growth = Initial Investment * Rate of Return

Investment Growth = $10,000 * 0.02

Investment Growth = $200

Now, the opportunity cost of choosing Option A over Option B would be the difference in returns between the two options:

Opportunity Cost = Potential Return from Option B - Actual Return from Option A

Opportunity Cost = $200 - $800

Opportunity Cost = -$600

In this example, by choosing Option A (investing in Stock X), you gained $800 but missed out on the opportunity to gain an additional $600 that you would have received if you had chosen Option B (investing in the Savings Account). This $600 is the opportunity cost of your decision.

Opportunity cost helps highlight the trade-offs involved in decision-making and reminds us that the resources we allocate to one choice come at the expense of potential gains from other choices.

4. Return on Investment (ROI)

Return on Investment (ROI) is a financial metric that measures the profitability of an investment relative to its cost. It's a way to assess how much you've gained from an investment compared to how much you initially put in. Here's a simple example to help illustrate ROI:

Imagine you invest $1,000 in shares of a company's stock. Over the course of a year, the value of your investment grows to $1,200. During that year, you also received $50 in dividends from the company. To calculate your ROI, you'd use the following formula:

ROI = [(Ending Value - Initial Investment + Dividends) / Initial Investment] × 100

In this case:

Initial Investment = $1,000

Ending Value = $1,200

Dividends = $50

Plugging these values into the formula:

ROI = [($1,200 - $1,000 + $50) / $1,000] × 100

ROI = ($250 / $1,000) × 100

ROI = 25%

So, in this example, your ROI on the investment is 25%. This means that for every dollar you initially invested, you gained an additional 25 cents in profit.

ROI is a valuable tool for evaluating the efficiency and profitability of investments. It allows you to compare the returns of different investments and assess whether they are worth pursuing. Keep in mind that while ROI provides a useful snapshot of an investment's performance, it doesn't take into account factors like the time period of the investment, the associated risks, or the potential impact of inflation.

5. Return on Asset (ROA)

Return on Assets (ROA) is a financial metric used to assess a company's efficiency in generating profits from its assets. It's calculated by dividing the company's net income by its average total assets. Here's a brief example:

Let's say Company XYZ reported a net income of $500,000 for the most recent fiscal year. During that year, their average total assets amounted to $5,000,000. To calculate ROA:

ROA = Net Income / Average Total Assets

ROA = $500,000 / $5,000,000

ROA = 0.1 or 10%

In this example, Company XYZ's ROA is 10%. This means that for every dollar of average total assets they had, they generated 10 cents of net income. It's a measure of how efficiently the company is using its assets to generate profits. A higher ROA generally indicates better asset utilization and profitability.

6. Market Value

Market value refers to the current price at which an asset, such as a stock, bond, real estate property, or commodity, can be bought or sold in the open market. It reflects the perceived worth of the asset based on the interaction between buyers and sellers in the market. Here's a brief example:

Let's consider a fictional company, ABC Inc., which is publicly traded on the stock market. As of today, the market price of one share of ABC Inc. is $50. This means that if you wanted to buy one share of ABC Inc., you would need to pay $50. Similarly, if you owned a share of ABC Inc. and wanted to sell it, you would receive $50.

This $50 represents the current market value of one share of ABC Inc. It's determined by various factors such as the company's financial performance, investor sentiment, economic conditions, and supply and demand dynamics in the stock market. The market value can fluctuate over time as these factors change, leading to changes in the asset's price.

7. Book Value

Book value, also known as "net asset value" or "carrying value," is the value of an asset as reported on a company's balance sheet. It's calculated by subtracting accumulated depreciation or amortization and any liabilities associated with the asset from its original cost or purchase price. Here's a brief example:

Imagine Company XYZ purchased a piece of machinery for $100,000 several years ago. The machinery's useful life is estimated to be ten years, and it has been depreciated at a rate of $10,000 per year. Additionally, the company has a liability related to the machinery of $20,000.

To calculate the book value of the machinery:

Book Value = Original Cost - Accumulated Depreciation - Liabilities

Book Value = $100,000 - ($10,000 * Number of Years Depreciated) - $20,000

If, for example, the machinery has been used for five years:

Book Value = $100,000 - ($10,000 * 5) - $20,000

Book Value = $50,000 - $20,000

Book Value = $30,000

In this example, the book value of the machinery after five years of use would be $30,000. It represents the asset's value on the balance sheet after accounting for its original cost, accumulated depreciation, and associated liabilities. It's important to note that book value doesn't necessarily reflect the market value or the true economic value of the asset, especially if market conditions or other factors have changed since its acquisition.

8. Business Cycle

The business cycle refers to the recurring pattern of economic expansion and contraction that economies experience over time. It consists of four main phases: expansion, peak, contraction (also known as recession), and trough. Here's a brief example to illustrate these phases:

Expansion: During this phase, the economy is growing, and key indicators such as GDP, employment, and consumer spending are on the rise. Companies are experiencing increased sales, and investors are generally optimistic about future prospects.

Peak: The peak marks the highest point of economic activity in the business cycle. It's characterized by full employment, high consumer spending, and often elevated inflation. Companies are operating at or near full capacity, and the economy is at its strongest.

Recession: In this phase, economic activity starts to decline. GDP growth slows down, unemployment rises, consumer spending decreases, and business investment contracts. This phase can lead to reduced economic output and negative growth.

Trough: The trough represents the lowest point of the business cycle. Economic indicators are at their weakest, and the economy is at its lowest level of output. Unemployment is high, and consumer confidence is low.

After the trough, the cycle starts anew with another expansion phase. The business cycle is a natural occurrence in economies and is influenced by a variety of factors, such as changes in consumer behavior, technological advancements, monetary policy, fiscal policy, and external shocks.

Understanding the business cycle is crucial for policymakers, businesses, and investors as it helps them anticipate and respond to economic changes and fluctuations.

9. Gross Domestic Product (GDP)

Gross Domestic Product (GDP) is a fundamental economic indicator that measures the total value of all goods and services produced within a country's borders over a specific period of time. It's often used to gauge the overall economic health and size of a country's economy. Here's a brief example:

Let's consider a fictional country, Econoville, for the year 2022. In that year, the country produced goods and services valued as follows:

Goods produced (such as cars, smartphones, and clothing):

$300 million

Services provided (such as healthcare, education, and entertainment): $200 million

To calculate the GDP of Econoville for the year 2022:

GDP = Value of Goods Produced + Value of Services Provided

GDP = $300 million + $200 million

GDP = $500 million

In this example, the GDP of Econoville for the year 2022 is $500 million. This figure represents the total economic output of the country during that year. GDP can be calculated on a quarterly or annual basis and is used to compare the economic performance of different countries, track changes in economic growth, and inform various economic policies.

10. Bear Market

The principle of a bear market is simple. Essentially, it represents a negative or pessimistic outlook on a stock market's performance, often with such markets falling into a downward spiral, where prices continue to drop.

As a result of a bear market, sales of stocks tend to increase. Additionally, investors expect increased losses from their investments.

11. Bull Market

A bull market represents a much more positive outlook on a stock market's performance compared to a bear market. In a bull market, stock prices either have or are expected to increase.

As a result of a bull market, purchases of stocks tend to increase. Additionally, investors expect increased profits from their investments.

Teaching yourself about money management can change your future and set you up for success in life. Today, the world is ruthless in financial matters, and lack of stability brings nothing but stress and misery. It damages the standard of living. However, becoming a financially literate person can keep you from making costly mistakes in life.

So, in this chapter, we have reached an understanding that

financial literacy is the key to a safe, secure, and happy future. However, the process of making oneself financially literate does not have to be scary or complicated. With just the right financial literacy skills, the young generation can learn how to manage their financial lives and grow into confident and successful adults.

Key Takeaways from This Chapter:

Chapter 1 of the book highlights the importance of financial literacy in today's world. The author claims that it's high time for people to understand the significance of financial literacy before they become overwhelmed by debt. The chapter suggests that if you start learning about financial literacy now, you could pass on generational wealth to your children instead of generational debt. The author encourages readers to dive into the world of financial literacy, which can help them learn new ways to save money and increase their income. Overall, the chapter urges readers to take financial literacy seriously, as it can significantly impact their financial future.

- The chapter talks about the fact that there is no appropriate age for financial literacy, and the earlier you start, the better result it will generate.
- Then, it proceeded to give accounts of prominent people like Michael Jackson and Mike Tyson, who lost all their wealth because they were not financially literate, emphasizing the fact that financial literacy should be mandatory in schools and colleges.

The chapter talks about what people, specifically the younger generation, are doing wrong, which includes,

- They take an uncalculated risk
- They try to get rich the quickest way possible.
- They don't educate themselves on money matters.

- They are impatient and don't invest slowly over time.
- They don't monitor their investments and leave them alone to mature.
- They are into using credit cards for convenience.

Towards the end, the chapter discusses the benefits of financial literacy and why it should be taken seriously.

- Ability to Make Better Financial Decisions
- Effective Management of Money and Debt
- Better Equipped to Reach Financial Goals
- Reducing Expenses and Investing
- Saving for Retirement and Emergencies

Chapter 2: The Psychology of Money

"Beware taking financial cues from people playing a different game than you are."

-Anonymous

It is commonly believed that if a person is book-smart or has a good IQ level, they are most likely to achieve great heights of success, especially when success is claimed to be directly proportional to money. Though there is no valid evidence to support this claim, just one click on any search engine can provide multiple results that can nullify this belief instantly. The reason is that achieving the desired wealth level is not about relying on the pre-existing knowledge of an author who was cremated long ago.

Indeed, it is important to have some prior knowledge, but at the same time, one needs to be highly street-smart to accumulate real wealth. Needless to say, the world is progressing rapidly. That explains why most self-made millionaires are either the ones who earned Cs in their academics or the dropouts from the most prestigious colleges. These people are also the ones who are more eager to learn the psychology of money than to rely on outdated, bookish content.

This is why if you ask for some expert advice from me, I must ask you to dig into your money-related tendencies. To be honest, we as individuals are wired differently. We all have different needs, which is obviously justified, but the thing is, we all prefer to have different spending thresholds without having any restrictions. A mindset like this could get the person in trouble if not ascertained at the correct time.

Let's take a day-to-day example to grasp the idea of the psychology of money and how it affects our daily lives. This brings us a step closer to financial motivation and what it tells about a person. Have you heard about *the safety vs. the status* way of spending? This is an outstanding way to determine the financial motivation of an individual. For instance, most people prefer to name a luxurious car not because they really fell for the model but because they were taught to associate huge brands and luxury items with success.

Now, ask yourself. What do you do when choosing safety vs. status while spending money? If you lean toward safety, then you are a person who believes in security, but if your answer is status, then it is a must for you to keep your spending in check. Indeed, going out of the way to get the branded belongings can make a person go broke before they realize it. They feel like they are purchasing happiness in exchange for money, but the truth is they are devaluing their hard-earned money.

Instilling a habit of valuing money by purchasing useless, luxurious brands can be daunting for some people, and why wouldn't it be? They have developed their whole personality around it; how can they change themselves overnight? It is not easy to bring sudden changes, especially when a person's whole personality is spiraled around it. Still, the good part is that taking little steps one by one can make it happen.

Here are the 5 Cs that can help an individual grasp the concept of money.

CLARIFY:

There is a very thin line that separates the poor from the rich, and that is the understanding of liabilities and how it is different from assets. But to my surprise, most people cannot distinguish between both terms. It is of utmost importance for every person to be able to determine where he stands financially. It should not be considered a bogus idea; instead, a person should clarify his income and what he owns while knowing his assets accurately.

CLASSIFY:

This is where you are required to divide your money in such a way that it fulfills your basic needs while ensuring you have some amount designated for investment. For instance, you choose to leave 40% of your earnings for your basic needs, while you take a small amount of 15% for entertainment. At the same time, ensure that your education and donation get at least a share of 2.5%, respectively, and the remaining 20% for your investment plan. It is significant to classify your earnings so that you do not end up bankrupt by the end of the day.

CATEGORIZE

Always remember categorizing the income is a must. One can never go wrong with categorizing his hard-earned amount into different small groups. People usually regard it as *budgeting,* but it is a life-saving hack for me. Budgeting is all about creating a monthly expense list where you learn to differentiate between your fixed and variable expenses. To me, budgeting is like a gentle reminder with a request telling you where exactly you should spend your money.

COUNT:

Now is the time to track your spending. You have already developed a budget that will help you stay on track, but this is only possible when the budget is implemented honestly. You can simply opt for a spending tracker to make the process easier. Additionally, tracking down spending is a great step in understanding your spending habits. This will make you shed light on the wasted spending pattern, making it easier to see what should be taken off next month's budget list.

COMMIT TO SAVING:

Spending money to show people how much money you have is the fastest way to have less money.

Many of us prefer to spend money not because we want to but because we want to appear as one of the richest. As previously mentioned, we associate our worth with money, and that is where the psychology of money comes in handy.

Spending whatever little amount of money you have for a short moment of happiness is not what makes you a valuable person. Trust me, this is not a rational mindset, and it can cost you an arm and a leg. On the other hand, saving a small amount from your income permits you to invest money whenever there is a right opportunity, but what if you have nothing saved up for yourself and an outstanding opportunity knocks on your door? This is the reason why committing to saving should never be neglected.

Clarify Where You Stand Financially

For some people, assessing their financial standpoint or clarifying their financial position might not be as simple. Others might not be sure of it. Mark my words. Clarifying your financial position is as simple as it appears to be. There is no rocket science in it.

So, how is it done?

Your financial health is calculated by learning about your *net worth,* but you do not have to fret over the technical terms. Net worth is the representation of the existing wealth, measured by the assets remaining after deducting what you owe to others. As I previously said, liabilities and assets are two entirely different concepts, and their differences should be rote-learned. Moreover, it is important to calculate your net worth accurately. To calculate the net worth, it is essential to list the assets and liabilities, and whatever the difference achieved is known as the net worth.

For the people who do not understand what assets are, it include things like your house, car, savings, jewelry, insurance policy, and even the cash value in the replacement of your life. In contrast, liabilities include the things that you owe to other people. For instance, mortgages, bank loans, credit cards, and so on. This is the starting point of your planning. If your net worth is positive, then it is a piece of good news for you. However, if you end up with a negative net worth, even then, you do not have to panic. Start building a plan, work on it, and get out of debt. It's never too late!

You must have heard the quote by Friedrich Schiller: *"The rich become richer, and the poor become poorer."* This stands true owing to people's little knowledge about what assets are and what liability could do to their future. Though both of these concepts are entirely different from each other, even to this day, the general masses cannot comprehend them on their own. This is one of the reasons why they usually misunderstand liability as an asset. At the same time, a wealthy person would be quick enough to calculate whether their assets are directly creating a money flow or are they a liability. Since not many middle and lower-class people are familiar with this concept, they get stuck with tons and tons of liabilities. These never-ending liabilities have turned every commoner into Sisyphus, where they are condemned to live the same life and earn the same amount of money to give it all to the bank.

Sisyphus was cursed and could not do anything to change his eternal wrath, but what about you? You can always bring change to your life, avoiding rash decisions. Suppose you have to relocate to a new place for job purposes, and you take out a loan to purchase a second home near your workplace. Now, here is the thing: you are indeed investing in assets, but the point is there is no cash flow. Instead, you keep paying your every penny to the bank; then, is it really an asset?

What you can do is rent one of your houses or apartments to credible people and ensure you receive a positive cash flow by the end of every month. This cash flow should be further invested wisely to generate a decent amount of passive income. This is how you improve your earnings, but with that, it is also important to instill an appropriate mindset within your family and social circle. Teaching them the psychology of money while teaching them a little about money management skills.

These days, it's common for people to have insufficient financial assets to retire, which means they don't have enough money to retire. It's not just the people on the brink of retirement who are in a bad financial situation. You would be surprised to know that 80% of the 27-year-olds are in debt. Most of them owe more than $10,000. This statistic makes it all the more important to start correcting the young generation and tutoring them about the psychology of money, how to value money, how to spend it, how to save it, and how to invest it.

Teaching the Young Generation About Money

1. Teach Them Contentment

The world has changed a lot, and there is no lie that the generation of this age goes through a lot more pressure than any of the previous generations. They have opened their eyes to the world of comparison, and before they realize it, they become part of it. They get seriously pressured if they do not have the latest PlayStation or if their house is not up to the mark. But let me tell you one thing: These kids will always feel this way even if you give them the whole world. They will always feel the void inside them because they started understanding material reality at an early age.

To help them get over this feeling, it is important to familiarize them with contentment. Believe it or not, this will lead them to a joyous life. Explain to your teens how living on a superficial level can bring doom to the family. Include them while you prepare a monthly budget. Make them understand the value of hard-earned money through your actions.

2. Make Them Aware of Credit Cards

It won't take long until your young one turns 18, and their phone will suddenly be bombarded by the multiple banks offering them credit cards. But before they get into the world of credits, it is your duty as an adult to make them conscious about not giving in to the credit temptations. Be open about the cons of credit cards and tell them why they should never become another victim of one.

3. Tell Them the Wonders of Compound Interest/Profit

You need to believe me when I say that your whole family and social circle should be well-equipped with the knowledge of compound interest. It can do wonders! Compound interest/profit possesses enough power to make your income double. It allows you to earn returns on the money you invest and the returns at the end of every compounding period. This is the major reason you should ask your family members to start saving, especially your children. Introduce them to the idea of saving at an early age, make them learn the benefits, and see them walking on the road to financial stability from a young age.

What the Young Generation Needs to Know

There is no doubt that people who start investing from an early age tend to be more successful in their lives than those who start late, yet there are still a few things that these young minds should be aware of.

1. Opportunity Cost

Forget young minds; most of the time, even adults are unaware that spending money has two costs. Simply put, when you purchase something, you pay its actual cost, and the other cost is the lost opportunity of purchasing something else with the amount of money you just spent. This money is no longer available; hence, the opportunity of buying the other thing no longer stands valid for you.

The idea of opportunity cost is important because when a buyer has to purchase any good, he will ask himself, "What will I be losing if I purchase this product?" This is not only restricted to major buyers, but even youngsters should pause before purchasing anything while ensuring they are not losing a great opportunity.

2. Commission

Parents love to pamper their children, and it should not be a problem until the children stop making an effort. This usually happens when parents prefer to give as much allowance as their kid asks for without realizing that it might end up spoiling them. Especially when they are teenagers, they should not be spoiled through allowance. Instead, providing a reasonable amount of money on completing specified tasks will give them a glimpse of the real world. This will also make them passionate about each assigned task since they are being paid. Besides, if it is their hard-earned cash, they will be more responsible while spending the money.

3. Budgeting

There are two key components to preparing a basic budget—income and expenses. Spending more money than you are making should always be a big no-no. Instead, the ideal condition is where you make more money while your expenses require spending less.

Most people live a full-stress life by spending more than what they earn, and to make ends meet, they take out multiple loans, but this does not make life any easier for them. Following a budget could provide aid in keeping your expenses in check. Plus, making the young generation learn how to budget can teach them all the essential traits required to survive in the real world.

4. Investing

As per Cooper's research, 32% of the young generation cannot tell the difference between a credit and a debit card. Additionally, they feel uncomfortable about their little financial knowledge because their adults lack financial literacy and never include them in any financial talks at home. They blindly repeat the myths like *it can wait till you grow older* without considering its consequences. The thing is, these adults themselves are unaware of the benefits that come with the investment, and so they lack the power to determine what is good for their children's future.

Investing is not something that can be done overnight. It is a long play and requires a long-term investment to receive the right opportunity for your portfolio to grow its value. You have more opportunities to invest in a well-diversified portfolio at a young age and fewer things to lose. Looking for a winning stock when you have a lot to lose is not a correct strategy; instead, you will be more at risk of going bankrupt.

Imparting financial wisdom to the young generation seems like the right thing to do. It's the initiative every household should take if they want to become a family that is responsible in matters of money and finances. Since this generation is the key to a more financially prosperous future, it is imperative to create awareness among them at the right time. It will be a slow revolution, but a revolution nonetheless.

The young generation is more than willing and eager to learn about money management skills. Thus, they should be directed toward knowledge (like this book) so they develop an understanding of the psychology of money, stay on the right track, save money, and invest it efficiently. At first, it could be a lot of work, but once they equip themselves with this priceless education, they will see the wonders themselves.

Key Takeaways from This Chapter:

Chapter 2 of the book "The Psychology of Money" discusses the importance of being street-smart when it comes to making an investment. The author emphasizes that while prior knowledge is essential, it is equally important to understand the psychology of money to become financially successful. According to the author, self-made millionaires are eager to learn about the psychology of money rather than relying solely on academic knowledge.

The author suggests that understanding our money-related tendencies is crucial for financial success. As individuals, we have different needs and preferences, but we all have different spending thresholds. We may run into financial trouble without proper understanding and management of our spending habits.

To illustrate this point, the author provides an example of the safety vs. status way of spending. Many people prefer to associate luxury items with success, not because they genuinely like the product but because they have been taught to associate them with success.

The chapter highlights the importance of understanding our individual money psychology, which can help us make better financial decisions. By understanding our motivations and tendencies, we can make informed decisions about spending and investing our money, ultimately leading to greater financial success.

It talks about instilling the healthy habit of finances while introducing the concept of 5Cs to the readers. These 5Cs include **Classify, Clarify, Categorize, Count, and Commit.**

By the end, Chapter 2 also introduced the idea of opportunity cost, commission, budgeting, and investing.

Chapter 3: Saving

"Once you really accept that spending money does not equal happiness, you have half the battle won."

-Ernest Callenbach

From time to time, I notice people spending a huge sum of their income on things that may not be of value to them. The ironic part is that they know this purchase would never bring them any good, so why do they make such a purchase? The answer is actually simpler than you think. As humans, we have learned to associate our happiness with material value. People get plushies as self-proclaimed therapy; they spend all their money on expensive cafes just because the ambiance is gram-worthy. But where does this road lead to? Slowly and gradually, they start pushing the limits of their credit cards, and later on, they resort to bank loans to pay off their credit card bills. At this point, it would be safe to say that it has become a matter of buzz solely.

But this sudden dopamine rush lasts for an extremely brief moment while the money and time you have wasted cannot be recovered at any cost. That is exactly why you start to reconsider your decision right after making a purchase. You can discern the faded vision of your dream life from a mile away now, and I am sorry to inform you that this distance will keep increasing if you do not bring any modifications to your spending style. Earning a good amount of money does not ensure any stability in life. You might be in an influential position right now, and with a six-figure salary, you might not be considering saving an option, but let's say you suddenly get laid off, then? How would you manage your expenses while being unemployed? You do not have savings, you already took a bank loan, and you have a credit card bill to pay. Let's not be delusional here. Everybody knows how temporary a job can be in the times we are living in now. You will think you are irreplaceable until somebody walks in as your substitute.

That is why you will find me so adamant about savings, and as an advocate of financial literacy, I take pride in promoting this idea. No matter how high your income is, there will be an end to it. Plan your savings wisely so that your hard work does not go in vain. Start saving today so that you do not have work until you are on the deathbed. Let's have a look into a few of the ways through which you can efficiently save money while not starving yourself.

1. Set Your Savings Goal

Most people believe that the right time to develop a saving goal is when you have reached a certain level of financial stability; however, they fail to realize that setting a saving goal is a must to achieve the said stability. If you choose to skip this step, you will surely miss out on the opportunity to live your dream life.

No matter if you are in your twenties, thirties, or maybe older, at this very moment, it should be your prime concern to set a saving goal. This is the time that you should start planning and saving for a better future.

2. Save for Emergencies

I could not stress this one enough. Always keep a separate fund for financial shock. This will stop you from relying on debts or loans. You can never predict an emergency, but you can choose to stay prepared if you encounter any unexpected circumstances. Emergency cash surplus will allow you to stay on track while not losing your entire savings in one go.

3. Save for Short-Term Needs

Short-term goals are your immediate expenses. These expenses are easy to achieve, and it takes around a year or two to accomplish them. This could include getting a new car, going on a trip, or maybe making minor home improvements. To save money for your short-term goals, it is essential to see where you stand financially and start planning accordingly. Determine how much money you should be saving and how much money is required to meet the basic necessities. You can start by preparing a budget while cutting down a little on your expenses. Moreover, you should try keeping track of your spending through a reliable tracking app. This will keep you motivated and make it easier for you to stay on your goal.

4. Save for Long-Term Needs

Long-term goals could get a lot more challenging since it requires planning for a longer duration. This may include paying off your mortgage, planning your kids' education, or starting a business. The wise approach is to take your short-term expenses into consideration before you set up any long-term goals. Saving money for long-term goals is a crucial step. It prevents you from going broke all of a sudden and provides you with a better and more secure future. However, saving for long-term goals is a lot more challenging than saving for short-term goals, but a little tolerance toward saving can help you eliminate all the barriers in your journey.

This reminds me of the real hindrances that stop people from saving a small sum of money from their earnings. Whenever I initiate a conversation regarding the significance of saving money, I have noticed people initially feel hesitant. Upon asking, they always come up with preconceived notions that stop them from having a little savings of their own. Honestly, this makes me want to bust all these myths instantly, so here I will refute a few saving myths still floating around.

Some Strange Myths About Saving

1. Saving is all about deprivation.

People believe saving equals being deprived of all happiness, which apparently is proportional to committing suicide, but that is not the case. Savings do not mean you will keep all your money intact until you get to breathe your last; instead, it is quite the opposite. You prepare for the future through savings, or as a wise financial analyst would argue, it brings us joy. In addition to that, saving money does not mean you will never get the chance to spend it. People tend to forget that it is still their money; they are the ones who will be spending this amount, but this time, they will make wise choices.

2. If I earn more money, saving will be easier.

This is a commonly shared myth. I do not know where it started, but somebody has to end it. We all know every human likes to take the bar of their spending high the first chance they get. Once you start earning more, your spending style will become lavish, and the day you start saving will never come. You will only indulge in spending more. Trust me, it won't do you any good. No matter how much money you make now, you will be left with nothing if you do not know how to secure it. Saving is never about having a huge sum to deposit in your bank account. It is about saving a small amount persistently and consistently.

3. I can only save a little bit, so it is not worth it.

It is always better to save a little amount while you can. This is far better than having nothing in your savings account and then taking out a bank loan. Besides, you might have heard that starting from somewhere is better than giving up completely. What if you can save a little for now? Your every penny will greatly benefit you when you require them in the future. It might be less at the moment, but there will be a time when it will become a river of wealth.

Also, saving a small amount of money is about instilling good financial habits. Once you learn to save money, you will get multiple chances to add a little more to your savings. Consider it as your first step toward financial freedom.

4. I will start saving money when I make more money.

I have heard people making such huge, hollow claims, but in my opinion, they try to hide behind these excuses. Yes, I would not prefer to call it a myth; instead, I feel it is more of an excuse that people came up with for their ease.

Now the question is, how would your earnings ever grow if you neither save nor invest it anywhere? Secondly, if you are up for an increment, even then, more earnings do not guarantee more savings. This projects a clear image of how you perceive money and what kind of financial mindset you have developed so far.

5. I can always get a loan if things go bad.

Ask yourself, can you? Would there be any bank that would loan you anything without any collateral or mortgage? Why would they? Banks are not non-governmental organizations that work selflessly to serve you. They need to keep their profit margin while ensuring you will pay them back as soon as possible. Approaching banks in dire straits will never benefit you in any way. This gives you many more reasons to stop believing recklessly in this irrational myth and to never opt for a bank loan, especially when you are going through a rough patch.

6. I want to be a good parent, so I need to give to my kids now so they can have a better life.

Every parent has this urge to fulfill the tiniest need of their children; however, when parents coddle their children a little too much, they rob them of becoming self-reliant, responsible citizens of this society. Their children slowly and gradually start feeling crippled and completely dependent on their parents. A study suggests that 5% of 18-24-year-olds get some form of economic help from their parents, and 40% get $10,000 or more a year. This also explains the attitude of boomerang kids who find it hard to survive independently and return to their parents' house after getting a first-hand experience of the real world. Therefore, rather than trying to fulfill every need of your kid, what you can do as a good parent is to help them become self-dependent.

"Self-reliance is the greatest gift any parent can give a child, for it is a habit of mind that follows him all his life and levels the mountains as he goes."

-Willard and Marguerite Beecher

7. You can only save when you are older.

There is no required age to start your saving journey. The earlier you learn to save, the better outcomes you will get. There are countless such stories where you will see people getting retirement at an early age. This is because these people were well-equipped with financial literacy, and they started saving in their twenties. Starting early means that you will get a lot more chances to learn and develop a proper skillset of financing while risking almost nothing. Starting to save early on in your life will also provide you with the essential tricks and put you in a better position.

The reason why most people blindly follow these myths is that they fear getting started with them. Saving requires discipline, tolerance, and sacrifices to some extent. Without these three elements, it is almost impossible to save efficiently.

Start Saving from Today!

A commonly argued notion is that saving money means being frugal, which, in all honesty, is a baseless idea. You do not have to be frugal to save money. Certainly, you can spend your income, but the ideal condition is you pay yourself and save first. Here is why you should jump on the start saving from today bandwagon:

1. Start Improving Your Financial Being

By developing a habit of saving, you are committing to a better future for yourself, and this is only possible if you choose to reduce your spending and cut your expenses. According to financial experts, spending beyond what you can afford and running up costly debt must be limited to lead a healthy financial life. Spending beyond your means can also distract you from your financial goals. However, listing your needs and saving a small amount can guarantee a secure future.

2. Saving Means You Can Take Calculated Risks

Building cash reserves so you can take calculated risks without stress is part of saving money. Moreover, pursuing certain passions may also be harder for you if you do not have savings. Let's suppose you want to start a business, for instance. However, even if you are a small business owner, you will need financial backing to get it off the ground. Setting an appropriate saving goal and contributing religiously to it every month can allow you to explore many more excellent opportunities. Initially, you might feel a bit impacted by it, but remember, it is for the greater good.

3. Retire Early

Statistically proven, people who start saving at a young age are the ones who get to retire early. These people started to think about their future dream life when they were just youngsters. They were the people with visions who got to achieve their goals because their thinking was twelve to twenty years ahead. Not to mention, saving today will bring you more benefits tomorrow. As your interest/profit accumulates, the interest/profit you receive will, in turn, generate even more interest/profit. That is the benefit of compound interest/profit, an intriguing and life-changing concept that we will discuss in Chapter 5.

4. To Live a Debt-Free Style

In today's world, it is rare to find people with no debt, especially when everybody uses a credit card for every minor purchase. However, people must realize that these small purchases consume all their hard-earned amounts. But if you choose to live below your means while adding a little amount to your savings, your world can change drastically. Furthermore, saving a small portion of your income will help you easily meet discretionary expenses.

Shedding light on the importance of saving money makes people mindful of how they should manage money. Again, managing money is not tantamount to living a life of a miserly. Just the habit of saving and adhering to a controlled spending pattern would suffice and make you a financially responsible and smart individual.

Remember, a penny saved is a penny earned. Consistently setting cash aside can allow you to enjoy greater security in your life while getting a lot more chances to explore new and better opportunities.

Key Takeaways from This Chapter:

In Chapter 3, the author discusses the issue of people spending their income on things that do not hold any real value. They attribute their happiness to material possessions and engage in frivolous spending, leading them to push the limits of their credit cards and resort to bank loans to pay off their debts. The author emphasizes that earning a high income does not guarantee financial stability, and it is crucial to save money to prepare for unforeseen circumstances such as job loss. The author advocates for financial literacy and promotes the idea of savings as a means of ensuring financial security. They stress the importance of planning savings wisely.

The chapter gives step-by-step guidance on how one can save efficiently, which includes,

- Save for Emergencies
- Set Your Savings Goal
- Save for Short-Term Needs
- Save for Long-Term Needs

The chapter also looks into some widely believed myths and refutes them. Some of these myths are,

1. I will start saving money when I make more money.
2. I can always get a loan if things go bad.
3. I will start saving money when I make more money.
4. Saving is all about deprivation.

The chapter concludes with the idea that one should not procrastinate when it comes to saving and should start saving from this very moment. It further stresses prioritizing saving over frivolous spending and learning to live within their means. The author encourages readers to start saving today, no matter how small the amount may be, to ensure a better financial future.

Chapter 4: Budgeting

"If we command our wealth, we shall be rich and free. If our wealth commands us, we are poor indeed."

-Edmund Burke

I have observed many people wandering around in pursuit of wealth, but to no avail. Let me give my two cents on it. Building wealth does not come naturally to anyone, yet everybody starts somewhere. Everybody has to start from somewhere. This is where the savings come in handy, but what if you do not have them ready when you need them the most? You will risk losing a once-in-a-million chance to get rich just because your vision was narrowed.

Given that, from the outset, setting a financial goal should be every person's priority. It is significant to keep a check and balance on your spending and simultaneously identify whether it is impulsive, emotion-driven, or intention-driven.

When spending intentionally, you make a mindful decision considering all the pros and cons. You make choices that reflect your values and needs instead of letting emotions or outside influences dictate what you buy. Intentional spending is a habit that benefits your wallet and the environment. This type of spending ideally includes investing to receive a greater profit.

On the contrary, impulsive spending or emotional buying is when you purchase whatever your heart desires without weighing the pros and cons. People with impulsive spending habits try to make huge spendings beyond their means and go to any extent to make such purchases. These people are generally the major target of manufacturers who intentionally make unnecessary, impractical products with a higher cost to manipulate the consumers into thinking they need them.

Financial experts strongly discourage this kind of behavior and suggest that it should not be taken as a mere habit. Impulsive buying is a serious issue that needs to be kept in check. Researchers further argue that impulsive buying is directly related to financial strain, making the person slide into unmanageable debt and over-dependence on multiple credit cards. However, one needs to realize here that this is not the kind of attitude we are born with. This is not an innate human capacity; certainly, none is born with it.

The concept of impulsive buying is something humans entirely create to satisfy the hollowness inside them. They have attached their happiness to material value. The greater the value of a brand, the more worthy they feel it is. This explains why researchers dissuade people from having impulsive buying habits. They believe it is neither healthy for your financial nor mental health and can leave a negative impact for a lasting period. Even if the people around you love to associate money with happiness, you should be wise enough to predict the catastrophic effects of impulsive spending; after all, it is a matter of your future that should not be compromised.

If you learn to spend more intentionally at this point, you will be able to live a comfortable life shortly; however, if your impulsive buying becomes stronger, you will be left with nothing but a significant amount of debt sprinkled with lifetime regret and half-achieved dreams of becoming rich.

Living on others' expectations was never part of the plan. Remember, you are working to build a better future for yourself and not to impress people who mean nothing to you. This explains why you should start thinking about changing your future immediately; as British novelist and playwright John Galsworthy said, *"You cannot have one if you don't think about the future."*

Spending Right Leads to a Better Tomorrow

It's no hidden secret: spending right leads directly to a better living standard, yet these itsy-bitsy expenses always weigh us down, and we end up spending more than we should. This is one of the most-heard excuses of all time, but remember, this is not the only one. Let's quickly look into the most common yet insignificant expenses of all time and how most of us justify them daily.

- It was on sale; I got it for half of the price.
- This is the best one I could get at this price, and I didn't want to lose the opportunity.
- There is a better product in the market, and what I own at home has become ancient.
- Everyone in my surroundings has this, so I should get one too, or people will think I am boring.
- I deserve to satisfy the urge to splurge.
- It is a must to own it in this date and age.
- It plays an important role in my line of work.
- It holds great value in the market and will benefit me in the near future.
- Staying up to date with the latest market trends is what everyone does.

Now, the real concern is, if these excuses are bogus, what are the real causes that stop people from cutting down their expenses? You might think that living cost alone is efficient in stopping people from living a good lifestyle; however, in most cases, it is not true. Instead, the primary reason why people can't seem to save money is that they are highly addicted to emotional spending. As previously mentioned, manufacturers of products and services take advantage of the consumers' sentiments and manipulate them through multiple advertisements.

However, this does not fall entirely on the manufacturers. Consumers are partially responsible for leveraging brands to play with their psychology. Let's take a look at some common ways that turn the consumer into the victim of emotional buying.

- This will help me in healing internally.
- I found it adorable, and it was relatively cheap.
- I have worked hard for it, so I deserve to spend every dime.
- Nothing was in my foresight then, so I thought it would be a good idea.
- People will find me lovable.
- People will become more tolerant toward me, and I will become a part of a particular group.
- It makes me feel empowered.
- People will start noticing me.

Now, you must wonder what the big deal is around these little expenses. Honestly, these expenses might appear to be a small part of our life; however, if you look closely, these tiny expenses prevent you from building a good amount of savings.

If you cannot come up with a good spending decision, you can never save enough to invest it anywhere, and ultimately, your future will remain the same, or in the worst-case scenario, it will go downhill if you end up with debt.

This is the core reason for having the right saving vs. spending mind. It is essential for a better future. This is when you need to take complete control of your spending while cutting down all non-essential expenses. Remember, you have a financial goal that can only be achieved if your finances are in your control and not the other way around.

As a financial expert, this is where I believe in creating a basic yet effective budget. A budget will help you keep track of your spending so that you don't have to ask yourself where all your money went by the end of the month. A budget is crucial in understanding where your money should go, where it should not, and how much of it could be saved.

Most people argue that budgeting is synonymous with financial constraints. This projects a rather negative image of budgeting. More importantly, it does not hold any truth. Budgeting is about keeping a check and balance on your expenses so that you do not live to see the day when you become financially dependent on someone else. Your budget does not have to be restrictive to show its effects. Instead, religiously preparing and following a budget can help you achieve financial stability.

The problem lies with people believing that budgeting must be a complex process, which is quite the contrary. Budgeting should be done on a simpler level following the basic budgeting steps. It is not a complex process and should not be treated like one. Instead, prepare a budget that could be adapted easily. Planning a budget will help you analyze how much money should be spent in a month and what good amount should be saved. This budget thing might not be fun for everyone, but believe me, it is how you keep your household in balance.

Selecting the System for Money Tracking

Nowadays, there are countless options available to prepare a budget, but the real deal is figuring out which works best for you, from having a ready-made template to going as basic as using paper and pen. Below are some proven ways to track your money efficiently and conveniently.

1. Personal Finances Apps

People who find making the budget hectic should definitely look into personal finance apps. Nowadays, there are tons of mobile-friendly apps available online that allow you to link the app with your credit cards while managing your expenses on the go. The good part is they automatically update your expenses, and you don't have to worry about categorizing everything separately. Instead, these apps have built-in features to categorize your expenses into bills and payments to be made separately. The cherry on top is that you can also generate a monthly report of your spending rate.

2. Spreadsheets:

Almost all of us have heard about Microsoft Excel. It is easily accessible and designed in a way that anyone can use it, be it a beginner or a professional. You don't have to be tech-savvy or professional with technology to prepare a budget in Excel. All you need to do is look for the templates, select the formulas, add your expenses, and do the calculations. With that, it will update everything from the amount spent and the amount left on its own while you add new entries.

3. Pen and Paper:

This is one of the classic ways of preparing a budget, and I would say it is the easiest one out of all the three options. The majority of people have paper and pens available at their disposal, and they don't need any internet access or a computer to make a budget.

Indeed, there are chances to lose your budget if it is on paper. However, this is an exception and only happens when a person is not careful enough. Do bear this in mind: preparing a budget with paper and pen is only effective when you don't have multiple accounts to manage. However, if you have more than one account, I suggest you prepare a budget using technological devices.

Making an Effective Budget in 4 Simple Steps

I can't stress enough if you want to live a life of comfort in the near future, you need to learn the habit of budgeting to save efficiently. You need to build a clear understanding of how much is being spent and where it is being spent. This is how you can work on it with convenience.

1. Figure Out All of the Generated Income

At this point, you need to be aware of your past spending first. Start by making a list of all the required things. This includes:

- Salary
- Any government benefits, like disability payments or employment insurance
- Interest or profit from savings accounts
- Dividends from investments
- Capital gains (what you earn when an asset sells for more than you initially paid for it)

2. Figure Out the Expenses

Mapping out your expenses plays a significant role in preparing an effective budget. You can easily figure out your expenses by preparing a list at the end of each month. This list may include the following:

- Rent or mortgage payments

- Utility bills
- Groceries
- Fuel cost or public transportation
- Credit card bills and other debt payments
- School fees for children
- Communication (phone, internet, cable, etc.)
- Entertainment (streaming subscriptions, ordering takeout, books, etc.)

3. Classify Your Expenses into Fixed and Variable

Fixed costs are the expenses that largely remain constant each month. This may include house rent, mortgage, education, child support, etc. On the other hand, variable expenses recur from month to month. Money spent on entertainment, groceries, or any unplanned event is included in a variable expense.

Variable expenses may be higher or lower from one month to the next, depending on the circumstances. After figuring out your variable and fixed expenses, assign a spending value to each category, beginning with fixed expenses.

4. Total Your Monthly Income and Expenses

Having a grip on your total earnings is among the most essential to everything mentioned above. If you want to reach financial stability, your earnings should be more than your spending amount. This way, you can start planning and saving a good amount for retirement. Besides that, you can also go for the

'50-30-20' budgeting rule in such a case. It is a convenient budgeting method that can help you to manage your money effectively.

What is the 50/30/20 rule?

No matter how you manage your expenses, whether through an app or other means, you will want to know where your money is going. That is how you can move forward in planning a monthly budget. But for some reason, people abandon budgeting because they apparently find it hard to prepare it on their own. However, following the 50/30/20 rule, budgeting becomes much more straightforward. The basic rule of thumb is to divide your monthly income (after-tax, if tax is applicable) into three spending categories: 50% for needs, 30% for wants, and 20% for savings or paying off debt. Simple!

If your income increases over time, a good strategy or idea to increase your savings while keeping your expenses the same would be to switch to 50/20/30 or 50/25/25. The aim is to increase monthly savings as much as possible.

Using Your Budget

After putting all the hard work into preparing the budget, now is the time to monitor and track the expenses accordingly. You can use the same app or spreadsheet for this purpose. Compare the expenses with the budgeted figure and generate your report on how it went for a month. Use this first month as a launchpad for the future.

An excellent way to record your spending is by keeping an eye on your daily expenses rather than waiting for the month to end. It will stop you from overspending. Additionally, this will allow you to detect any problematic spending patterns if you have any.

Revise Your Budget

A budget is one of the most personal things one creates; however, life is unpredictable, and simply having a budget isn't enough. With time, life changes, and you start prioritizing different things. You need to revisit your budget every so often to make sure it still works for you. Make sure it aligns well with your current life goals.

Monitor Your Spending Habits

Most of the time, people shop for the things they want and not the things they actually require. This makes them go overboard, and they lose track of their spending. Monitoring your spending habits from time to time can help you understand your spending pattern, making it easier for you to spend while staying within your budget. Financial experts highly recommend keeping a close watch on your spending and creating a budget.

Without a budget, you will likely lose control over your spending. You might end up with tons of loans, but following a budget can do wonders for you. It allows you to understand the unhealthy spending pattern.

Using a realistic budget to forecast your spending can help you with your long-term financial planning while keeping your finances in order.

Key Takeaways from This Chapter:

Chapter 4 emphasizes the importance of realizing the catastrophic effects of impulsive spending on one's future, which should not be compromised. The author claims that it is not healthy for both financial and mental health and can leave a lasting negative impact. The manufacturers intentionally make unnecessary, impractical products with a higher cost to manipulate the consumers into thinking they need them, and people with impulsive spending habits try to make huge spendings beyond their means and go to any extent to make such purchases.

The chapter suggests that spending right can lead to a better tomorrow and illustrates the excuses a consumer uses to justify bad spending habits.

These excuses contain:

- It was on sale; I got it for half of the price.
- This is the best one I could get at this price, and I didn't want to lose the opportunity.
- There is a better product in the market, and what I own at home has become ancient.
- Everyone in my surroundings has this, so I should get one too, or people will think I am boring.
- I deserve to satisfy the urge to splurge.
- It is a must to own it in this date and age.

- It plays an important role in my line of work.
- It holds great value in the market and will benefit me in the near future.
- Staying up to date with the latest market trends is what everyone does.

After that, it talks about how consumers are emotionally and psychologically trapped in consuming expensive products.

- This will help me in healing internally.
- I found it adorable, and it was relatively cheap.
- I have worked hard for it, so I deserve to spend every dime.
- Nothing was in my foresight then, so I thought it would be a good idea.
- People will find me lovable.
- People will become more tolerant toward me, and I will become a part of a particular group.
- It makes me feel empowered.
- People will start noticing me.

As the chapter progresses, it introduces the idea of budgeting and how it could be done efficiently. Furthermore, it discusses the relevant ways to track money, for instance, personal finance apps, spreadsheets, and pen and paper.

Lastly, it comes up with four critical steps to prepare a budget.

- Figure Out All of the Generated Income
- Figure Out the Expenses

- Classify Your Expenses into Fixed and Variable
- Total Your Monthly Income and Expenses

Chapter 5: Debts

Debt is like any other trap, easy enough to get into but hard enough to get out of.

-Josh Billings

I am sure most of us have never heard about the term millennial burden in our lives, but I can also assure you that either one of us bears witness to this concept or has already become a victim because of multiple debts.

I would like to connect the concept of the millennial burden with the calamity of student loan debt, which, according to Forbes' 2023 Student Loan Debt Statistics, now stands at over $1.6 trillion. Student loan debt has grown to be one of the primary sources of consumer debt among millennials today, with more than 44 million people drowning in debt daily. Undoubtedly, millennials have become the unlucky generation constantly trying to contend with debts while facing economic anxiety simultaneously.

This being said, the new generation still has plenty of time to learn from the experiences of the previous generation so that they don't become the culprit of financial anxiety like the former one.

Given that, let's look into the conventional meaning of debt, its types, and the distinction between good and bad debts so that you don't go through the same financial anxiety as millennials.

Debt and Its Negative Implications

At its simplest, debt is when a party or company borrows money to make significant investments that are generally unaffordable and must be repaid with interest/profit within a certain amount of time. Mortgages, loans, credit card debt, and personal loans are the most common types of debt. Depending on the type of debt you have chosen, it can either be a helpful tool or become lifelong baggage.

On the surface, all debt appears evil, but let me tell you a little secret about financial advisors. Where they generally consider debt a bad idea, they classify it into two distinct categories: good and bad debt. As their names suggest, you can tell one debt will extract the maximum benefits for you, and the other will pull the full benefits out of you. That is why, as a financial expert, I encourage more and more people to get well-acquainted with good and bad debts.

Good Loan vs. Bad Loan

A good loan is borrowed money that is utilized to purchase items having a long-term value. For instance, consumers can borrow money to make these essential investments when they can't afford to pay cash upfront for education, a home, or a car. Good loans can also be utilized similarly in a company. For instance, business owners can invest in the future expansion of their company by using borrowed funds to purchase crucial supplies.

On the contrary, a bad loan is a type of debt that doesn't help your financial situation over time. High or fluctuating interest/profit rates and additional fees are common characteristics of less advantageous debt, showing the potential risk of trapping people in debt cycles.

How to Differentiate Good Loans from Bad Loans?

One thing about bad loans is that they never offer favorable interest/profit rates, unlike good debts with little to no fees. People usually take a good loan for the betterment of their future. This is more like an investment to get better outcomes; however, bad loans are mainly available to fulfill the short-lived luxuries with a high interest/profit rate.

Certainly, debts should not be approached as entirely evil. They are simple tools that should be used efficiently for ease and by ease. That does not mean you should take out loans to cover your occasional expenses. Instead, it should be used for things like mortgages or education that will impact your future for the better.

As I have always said, a healthy debt could help you sustain your business; however, taking out a microloan to secure funding would likely lower your net income. That's why microloan is widely seen as a ghost of a debt world that will haunt you forever.

Consequently, you should also know the kind of debt you are getting yourself into and whether it aligns well with your requirements. Here are the five kinds of debts that will help you develop your financial competence in loans.

1. Personal Loan

Personal loans are used for various things, such as paying off debt and covering medical costs. If a person needs money instantly, personal loans can serve their best interest as some lenders can put cash into your account as soon as the following business day. Additionally, rates, on average, are frequently lower than those on several other types of debt, such as credit cards.

However, it would be best to understand that personal loans, like any financial instrument, have disadvantages. For instance, some lenders have hefty fees, which significantly raise the cost of borrowing. Before taking out a loan, you should examine the benefits and drawbacks to decide if it's the right financing option.

2. Student Loan

Taking out a student loan can be a fantastic way to pay the college fee without going on breaks. The good part is that a student loan can easily be obtained from private lenders or the federal government. Most people prefer federal student loans due to their forbearance nature. These loans typically do not require a credit check and are provided as financial aid by schools and funded by the Department of Education.

On the other hand, private lenders typically require a credit check for student loans, while the terms and conditions are always different for every lender.

3. Mortgage Loan

Have you ever thought about purchasing your own house but then had to drop the idea because you could not get the funds? This is precisely where mortgage loans are handy for an average man who couldn't dream about making such a big purchase.

Through a mortgage loan, you can borrow money to finance what is likely to be the largest purchase of your life. Indeed, people love to see it as a home loan. Moreover, mortgage loans offer various options for various borrowers, including first-time homebuyers and military veterans.

4. Auto Loan

An auto loan is taken out to purchase a new vehicle while putting the newly purchased vehicle up as collateral for the lender; this is what makes the loan secure and closed-ended.

Typically, auto loan terms range from 36 to 72 months. However, as auto prices rise, longer loan terms are becoming more common.

5. Credit Builder Loan

A credit-builder loan does not require a credit check. Its objective is to assist individuals with poor credit or no credit file to improve their credit. The loan amount, typically $300 to $1,000, is deposited into a savings account by the lender. Then, you are asked to make payments in one lump sum every month for six to twenty-four months. Your payments are reported to at least one major credit bureau. This helps build your credit score.

A typical loan involves the borrower receiving the funds initially and paying it back over time. However, with a credit-builder loan, the lender retains the entire loan sum while the borrower makes payments. The borrower is given the total loan amount when all payments have been made.

Credit builder loans work best when you do not have pre-existing credit and are not in a rush to build up your credit scores. However, if your employment is not stable, it might not be your best option.

6. Debt Consolidation Loan

Many financial advisors consider debt consolidation loans a great way to pay a high-interest debt, especially credit cards. A debt consolidation loan will allow you to save money, given that the interest rate on the loan is lower than the interest/profit rate on your existing debt.

But what is the point of taking a loan to pay off another loan? Well, getting rid of your loan through a debt consolidation loan can lower your credit utilization ratio and raise your credit score.

However, as much as it is critical to learn about the types of loans, it is equally significant to look into the leading source of debt. As Northwestern Mutual's 2018 Planning & Progress Study suggests, the credit card is still in the top place in the debt market.

Another survey conducted by Select and Dynata claims that nearly half (44%) of 18 to 34-year-olds feel like they are "drowning in debt due to excessive credit card use, but they no longer have control over it.

Keeping this in mind, I have devised the following grounds to elucidate why you should stop swiping your card on every small purchase and start considering other factors.

1. Credit Cards Discourage Self-Control

Most people fail to understand that exercising restraint on your spending style is not a punishment but a way to pave the road toward financial stability. Still, most of us prefer having a fleeting moment of happiness over long-term satisfaction. They are unwilling to exercise self-control, and in the end, they get no other option but to put their financial stability at stake.

With credit cards, you start spending impulsively since you are no longer required to keep the balance in check. This sudden change in your attitude towards buying robs you of financial stability while negatively impacting your self-esteem and interpersonal relationships.

2. Using Credit Cards Means You Don't Have a Budget

Using a credit card might be fun and games until you realize you are not really spending money; instead, you are borrowing money. This implies that you neither have financial planning nor a set budget to live a stable life.

A budget is crucial in sustaining your current finances while constantly saving a small amount to chip in. Additionally, budgeting is a great way to track your expenses, but for people with credit card addiction, tracking becomes almost impossible, and they often end up with pretty bad credit.

3. Credit Card Interest/Profit Rates Are Expensive

Have you ever looked into the annual interest/profit rate of an average credit card? If not, you should refrain from making a purchase until you do your proper research.

On average, the interest/profit rate stretches beyond a 20% annual percentage rate, far higher than mortgages or auto loans. This makes your purchase three times more expensive than its actual cost. This amount may be negligible for some people, but it can cost you in the long run.

The guarded way to make a purchase is when you find a thing beyond your means, you should hold back from purchasing it. It is better than relying on credit cards that have exorbitant interest/profit rates.

4. Rates Rise When You Have Unpaid Balances

You might think that your credit card's annual percentage rate (APR) will stay constant. For the record, credit cards feature variable APRs that fluctuate with a specified benchmark, such as the prime rate. Therefore, your APR will be 16% if the prime rate is 4% and your credit card charges the prime rate plus 12%.

The problem is people firmly believe this will never happen to them, and they will be able to clear the tabs from time until they are knocked down by the unpredictable nature of life and get stuck with bad debt.

5. Credit Card Debts Can Ruin Your Relationships

Trust me or not, having bad credit can be a deal breaker in your personal life. If you have poor financial management skills, it will kill your stable relationship for sure. This is because credit card debt is often perceived as the accumulation of day-to-day decisions and highly reflects a person's competency to manage their finances efficiently.

In marriages, this is widely observed to be a reason behind a lower satisfaction rate. It also takes an emotional toll on the relationship, making it toxic for both partners.

6. Unnecessary Spending

Paying with a credit card feels like you are not spending real money. This means you will be fully convinced to get anything and everything since swiping a card satisfies you. This is because money is a tangible paper with some material wealth attached. Additionally, you do not have a spending limit at this point, so you will more likely link this feeling with financial freedom. This is how credit cards are designed so that they can play with your psychology. For a month, you will feel pain-free with no bills to pay, but the real struggle starts after that.

7. Credit Can Lead to Bankruptcy

While making any purchase on credit, people do not consider the risk of debt attached to it. For instance, you made a few purchases on your credit card while your circumstances were favorable, but let's say you lost your job at that very instant; how will you pay the remaining outstanding obligation? You will have to file for bankruptcy, which will badly impact your credit history. This will make you financially unstable and screw up your mental peace while leaving your family ties broken.

Considering all the factors, spending through credit cards is not worth losing so many things. A careful and sensible person would pay heed before charging on credit cards. Instead, they would better want to wait for the right time when they have the right amount of money to avoid the chances of going into debt.

Again, this might not seem like a big issue to some people. Others might consider it a piece of cake, which could be true in most scenarios, but every human should stay prepared for the worst-case scenario. Not being able to pay the debt on time can destroy your life for several years. A credit card can be perceived as a convenient mode of payment; however, the risks attached to it should not be ignored at any cost.

How to Cultivate Healthy Spending Habits

This generation is susceptible to falling prey to credit cards and their high interest rate. They seek comfort and convenience and are observed to be vulnerable while swiping their credit cards. But the real concern is if you are not tracking your spending, it will put your finances at risk. Given that, it is of utmost importance to shed light on the potentially growing problem for the betterment of youngsters. For that, it is advised to instill the significance of healthy spending habits while discouraging the use of credit cards.

It is crucial to cultivate healthy spending skills to sustain a strong credit score. This way, you can apply for a home loan or mortgage without hassle.

For your convenience, I have come up with five simple, easy-to-follow pieces of advice through which you can change your spending habits.

1. Prepare a Monthly Budget

A budget is prepared with the intention of channeling resources so that you can spend them on the things that should be given priority and not on the unlucrative ones. However, it might be a little off-putting for some people who associate it with a frugal lifestyle. Let me be precise: budgeting is not about restricting your spending; instead, it is the only way you can spend smart.

Creating a budget and sticking to it will allow you to use your monthly income to pay for all your costs while simultaneously keeping track of your hard-earned money. Nonetheless, if you do not prepare and adhere to a monthly budget, you will question where all your money went by the end of the month and will be forced to pay through a credit card even for the fixed expenses.

You do not have to worry about jotting down every small budget detail. Understandably, you might be short on time, which is fine. You can start from the basics. All you need to do is keep a log and record every expense of yours. Make sure to keep tracking your budget so you don't end up blowing it.

2. Reduce the Use of Credit Cards

Rick Gregory once said, *"It is sad that we have to gain control of the artificial numbers placed upon us by others to regain some control of our lives?"* I believe this is the reality of the new generation. They have a material value for everything, and they highly depend on making costly purchases through credit cards to satisfy their hollowness.

As aforementioned, credit cards are supposed to be used for emergency purposes; however, giving in to the temptation of swiping your card for the things you should have paid with cash could get you in serious trouble. That's why owning a credit card does not mean you should become a big spender. Instead, it would be best to learn to reduce spending while paying with a credit card.

3. Reduce Impulse Buying

While the advent of digital avenues for shopping has created ease for people, it has also opened the door for impulsive, on-the-spur-of-the-moment buying. And with a credit card at their disposal, there's nothing stopping people from spending excessively. Since you are not paying in cash for any purchase you have made so far, you will have to keep monitoring your spending before you lose track of it. This is critical because impulse buying could result in negative spending habits and drain a savings account if not managed correctly.

An easy way to control your impulsive buying is by leaving your credit card at home before shopping and taking limited cash along. This will allow you to spend money while staying within the limit. Alternatively, you can try thinking for a week before making any purchase to see if you want it in the fleeting moment or if it is an intentional purchase.

4. Look for Ideal Prices

I have always encouraged investing in the asset; this is the right choice, but one should learn to make sound judgments when making a big purchase, such as a car or house. They should know market trends and make conscious decisions when negotiating prices.

Just a tip: Don't forget to look into refurbished items; you might get lucky with them.

5. Focus on Your Goals and Think of Your Future

Sticking to a budget while cutting on most variable expenses might make you feel caged. But to fight the urge to spend excessively, you must keep the big picture in mind. You will have to keep reminding yourself why you started it first. Trust me, this way, it will be easier for you to stay on track while staying loyal to your future goal.

Keeping up with life's sudden changes may be difficult if your finances are out of order. Therefore, staying proactive and focusing on your goal is something I, as a financial expert, always promote. In a nutshell, the first step towards improving your finances is avoiding bad choices with a high consequential financial liability attached to them while sticking to your financial goal.

Key Takeaways from This Chapter:

Chapter 5 highlights the threat that debt poses to our upcoming generation as it reports the Forbes' 2023 Student Loan Debt Statistics and talks about how student loan debt has grown to be one of the primary sources of consumer debt among millennials today, with more than 44 million people drowning in debt daily. It begins with the millennial burden and points out their mistakes, making them the unlucky generation trying to contend with debts while facing economic anxiety simultaneously. Taking this into account, the author emphasizes that the new generation still has plenty of time to learn from the experiences of the previous generation to avoid becoming the culprit of financial anxiety like the former one. Therefore, the chapter focuses on debt, its negative impacts, and the distinction between good and bad loans. The final section consists of the means through which healthy spending habits can be stilled,

- Prepare a Monthly Budget
- Reduce the Use of Credit Cards
- Reduce Impulse Buying
- Look for Ideal Prices
- Focus on Your Goals and Think of Your Future

Chapter 6: Compound Interest / Profit

"Compound interest is the eighth wonder of the world."

-Albert Einstein

Once, Albert Einstein was asked about the most powerful thing existing on this earth, and he reputedly replied, "Compound Interest." Indeed, some people would call it a huge claim; some would even avoid the topic because its nitty-gritty details are hard to comprehend. But take my word for it... Once you get acquainted with the immense knowledge of compound interest/profit, it will do wonders for you. Given that, I have decided to shed light on this great topic so that more and more people can turn to compound interest/profit for a better life.

Let me start by saying that it is about time people start accepting that a retirement plan does not necessarily have to do anything with older age. Instead, the earlier you begin planning for retirement, the better it will be. However, the major concern is that having little savings does not guarantee a better life. It surely guarantees a failed plan for retirement. Putting all the savings as spare cash means you are more likely to lose on potential opportunities to grow your money. This is exactly why I advocate the significance of compound interest/profit, especially to the younger generation.

While this generation is a step ahead in technology and believes everything can be learned through the internet, they feel hesitant about acknowledging their lack of financial savviness. Most of the younger generation sees being financially savvy as being a wizard of the financial world, which is an overstatement. Having the basics of financial knowledge is not equivalent to being a financial nerd.

As per the 2022 survey of Investopedia financial literacy, 40% of the Gen Z population (the generation of people born in the late 1990s and early 2000s) is financially illiterate and does not understand the benefits of compound interest/profit and how it can improve their lives. Another report at George Washington University suggests that only one-third of Americans understand how compounding works, leaving most of the public in the dark.

This could be because people generally run away from complex things, precisely from the things that include formulas. But I would rather call it an ineffectual attempt that will ruin your life for good. Compound interest/profit does involve a formula, but trust me, it does not include complex derivations that used to haunt you in your school life.

So, without intriguing your curiosity, let's look into compound interest/profit, how it can be counted, and how you can use it efficiently for your benefit so that you don't end up financially unstable once you retire.

What Is Compound Interest/Profit?

With compound interest/profit, you do not just earn returns on the money you invest. You also earn returns on those returns as well at the end of every compounding period. The compounding period can be daily, monthly, quarterly, semiannually, or annually.

The concept of compound interest/ profit is significant in the world of finance since it allows your money to grow faster than simple interest/profit.

Now the question is, how would that work for you?

Well, the baffling part is compound interest/ profit allows you to earn interest/profit on previously earned interest/profit. Yes, you have read it correctly. But how so? The interest/profit you receive is calculated on the interest/profit accumulated over time and on the principal amount of your investment. This way, your original investment and the income earned grow together.

A common myth suggests that compound interest/profit requires a huge amount at first; only then could you accumulate some considerable wealth. That's not true! You do not need to invest an insane amount of money; instead, it is a matter of whatever you choose to invest. Besides that, if you want to learn how long it will take for your money to get doubled, all you need to do is follow the Rule of 72, and you will have your answer. Then again, what is the Rule of 72?

You might fret a little with all the mathematical stuff, but believe me, it is the easiest and quickest formula widely used to estimate the number of years required to double the invested money at a given annual rate of return. All you are required to do is divide 72 by the expected rate of return. Here is an example: If you made an investment that yields a return of 6% annually, you would double your investment in about twelve years. Remember, the bigger the initial investment is, the greater the return you will get.

However, one thing I would like to address here is you can never restrict investment to money only. All my life, I have noticed people presuming it only requires money. An entirely false belief that should be abandoned immediately. You must learn to invest your *time* and *money* to get into compound interest/profit. A little tip here. If you are willing to spend more time, you will save more by spending less. This is a little secret that not everybody will tell you because it holds immense power and can change your future for good.

So, you should be clear on the importance of investing from an early age.

Now, how about we look a little at the differences between compound and simple interest/profit in order to spare you from confusion?

How is Simple Interest/profit different from Compound Interest/profit?

Simple interest/profit is an interest/profit charge that borrowers pay lenders for a loan. It is calculated using the principal only. This type of interest/profit does not just relate to certain loans. Simple interest/profit is also the type of interest/profit that banks pay customers on their savings accounts.

On the contrary, when interest/profit is compounding, it means that in the next interest/profit period, the total balance (principal and interest/profit earned in the previous period) will be taken into account rather than just the principal. The next year, the interest/profit will be applied to the principal amount and the cumulative interest/profit earned, and so the compounding will continue. By compounding the principal sum's interest/profit, the entire principle aims to generate high returns. As someone very wise said, *"Money makes money. And the money that money makes, makes money."*

For short-term consumer loans like vehicle loans, simple interest/profit is frequently employed to compute the interest/profit. However, the interest/profit on credit card debts is compounded, which is why the debt seems to grow quickly.

The Key Factors of Compound Interest/Profit

Here are some critical factors that should be considered while calculating compound interest. Bear in mind all these factors show great significance on your investments, and a few of these variables can drastically affect the end product.

1. Interest/profit: This is the rate of interest/profit that you pay or earn. This implies that the higher the interest/profit rate, the more you earn or owe.

2. Principle Amount: The principal amount is the money you deposit or borrow.

3. Frequency of Compounding: The compounding period affects the rate of growth of your balance. It could be every day, every month, every half year, or every year.

4. Duration: How long will you hold money in a savings account? Alternatively, when will you pay back the loan? The longer you keep money in a savings account or hold a debt, the longer it will take for the money to grow and the more you will earn or owe.

5. Deposits or Withdrawals: How frequently will you make deposits to your account? How frequently will you pay back the loan? In the long run, a lot depends on how quickly you pay off your debt or increase your principal sum.

Compound Interest/Profit Formula

Some people would claim that knowing the formula for compound interest/profit is not really important since everything can be calculated through online sources; however, as an expert on financial literacy, I would claim being acquainted with the formula and learning the factors that affect compound interest/profit should never be neglected. The formula helps you understand the workings of compound interest/profit.

Compound interest/profit can be calculated by virtue of this formula:

$A = P(1 + [r/n])^{\wedge} nt$

Where:

A is the amount of money accumulated after n years, including interest/profit.

P is the principal amount (this can either be your initial deposit or your initial credit card balance).

r is the annual rate of interest/profit (use the decimal figure).

n is the number of times the interest/profit is compounded per year.

t is the number of years (time) for which the amount is deposited or borrowed.

The annual interest/profit rate is divided by the number of times it is compounded every year. This way, depending on the frequency of compounding, the calculation shows you the daily, monthly, semiannual, or annual interest/profit rate. For a better understanding, let's take an example here. Suppose you deposit $10,000 into a savings account that pays 5% interest/profit every month for ten years. In this example, you have P (10,000), r (0.05), n (12), and t (10). A is what you need to calculate. So, this is how the working will look like:

A = P (1 + [r / n]) ^ nt
A = 10,000 (1 + [0.05 / 12]) ^ (12 * 10)
A = 10,000 (1.00417) ^ (120)
A = 10,000 (1.64767)
A = 16,470

This calculation shows you will have $16,470 in your account in ten years. This includes your initial $10,000 deposit and $6470 interest/profit earned.

Besides that, **Microsoft Excel** works just fine as well when it comes to calculating compound interest/profit. It would help to utilize the Future Value (FV) function for that. Here's how you can do this calculation:

=FV(rate,nper,pmt,[pv],[type])

Where:

FV is the future value.

rate is the interest/profit rate per period.

nper is the total number of times interest/profit is calculated.

pmt is the additional money you add each period.

pv is the present value or the initial deposit. If you omit this, it's assumed to be 0.

type is either the number 0 or 1. 0 indicates payments are due at the end of the period, whereas 1 indicates payments are due at the start of the period. If you omit this, it's assumed to be 0.

When you intend to make additional deposits to your account, it is simpler to perform calculations in MS Excel. However, the calculation will produce the same outcome as the initial equation if the *pmt* variable is not used. If you intend to add $100 per month to your initial investment of $10,000, the following is how your compound interest/profit will be affected.

=FV(0.05/12,10*12,100,5000,0)

After ten years, with 5% interest/profit, you will have about $31,998 in your savings account.

However, you need to understand one important lesson here. Where compound interest/profit is your ally, it can also become your worst enemy, especially where the loan is concerned. This indicates that the amount you must pay will increase either monthly or annually, depending on the frequency with which your loan is compounded. Interest/profit on your loan will increase the longer you delay repayment.

For instance, you have a $10,000 loan for five years with an annual interest/profit rate of 5%. Using the aforementioned methods, you can see that if you pay off the loan in three years, you will have to pay $1,576 in interest/profit. Furthermore, assuming you take care of the advance in five years, you will owe $2,763 in interest/profit.

Learn the Magic of Compound Interest/Profit

Here are certain tips through which anyone can easily make compound interest/profit work for them.

1. Give Yourself Some Time:

In this book, I repeatedly stressed that saving and investing should be done from an early age. As a popular saying goes, *save for retirement.* Start from your first paycheck. There is no age for saving and investing. The earlier you start, the higher the results are. Compounding your money early on will enrich you with greater benefits, while retirement savings will also grow.

2. Pay Off Debts Quickly:

Build the habit of paying debts aggressively. If you take longer to pay your debts, all your hard-earned money will be wasted. Whether you took a student loan or need to clear the tabs for your credit cards, make sure you pay it as soon as possible.

3. Compare APYs:

The annual percentage yield (APYs). It will give you a more precise idea of what you will earn or pay in interest/profit than the annual percentage rate (APR). That's because APR is for simple interest/profit, and APY is for compounding.

4. Check the Compounding Rate:

I believe all of us would want our savings to compound more frequently and debts to compound infrequently. For that, try keeping track of compounding rates. It will greatly affect the amount you will earn or owe.

Can You Retire a Millionaire?

It should come as no surprise that retirement planning is serious business, and I have witnessed people dreading it. Certainly, I understand making a will, deciding when to take social security benefits, having to meet Medicare deadlines, and outliving your savings include this fear, and that's why I strongly voice my concern about early savings and investment. When you're young, you feel there is a lot of time and find it hard to think that far ahead. Besides that, many things can change over time, but planning now will help you take early retirement from your tiring life, not as a bankrupt person but as a *millionaire!*

Apparently, some people would perceive it as an empty suit, but for others, it's a reality. All you need to do is develop a strategic plan and decide how much savings you need to reach your desired goal. Using estimates as well as the 4% rule, you could take about $40,000 out of that balance each year. At first, some people may find this amount insufficient. The next step is to put the savings into investment. Remember, you save money to put into investments. If your amount is lying in the bank, it will grow at a steady speed. There are also chances that your bank might grow broke before you do. Considering this, do not let your money rot in your bank account; instead, invest it efficiently to take early retirement without fearing you will outlive your savings.

Let's quickly do a rough calculation to find an estimated amount a person can save for retirement through investment. For this purpose, I am taking a hypothetical investment period of forty-five years and a retirement age of 65. With that, I am calculating the investment needs of a person as young as 20 so that the young generation can be influenced. Moreover, I am assuming a 9% average annual return on the money.

If you look closer, a while back, reaching a million dollar amount was almost impossible, but after all the calculations, you can tell this is the easiest achievement for a 20-year-old to attain in forty-five years' time by the age of 65. Following the assumption above and using the compound interest/profit formula mentioned earlier, a 20-year-old would need to save and invest $136 each month to reach a million dollars by retirement. He will be able to save an amount of $1,007,063 after forty-five years, though his total investment was $73,440 in all these years. This shows how much power compound interest/profit holds.

Here is a lead to achieving your goal a little faster. Due to rising inflation, the value of your money will keep going down, but the antidote is to continue increasing your savings amount little by little daily, and you will not regret it.

If and only if I made the young generation feel overwhelmed with all the big digits talk, here is another angle to consider that will make saving much easier. Each week, you are saving just $31.15 or $4.44 each day. Now, question yourself: Can't you manage to save this little amount daily or weekly for a better future?

Here's another example. If a person starts saving at the age of 30 with the intent to reach a million dollars by retirement at 65, he will have to save and invest approximately $340 per month. Yet, even though it is better to save earlier, planning to retire a millionaire at 30 years of age is still not that bad, and you are still likely to attain the desired goal. If you start at 40, the amount to save and invest would obviously increase, but the good news is that you still have more time now than next year or the year after that, even if you didn't start early.

This is why I always say compounding does wonders for everyone, and a person with wit would never let such an amazing opportunity pass by without taking full advantage of it.

Key Takeaways from This Chapter:

Chapter 6 of the book focuses on compound interest/profit and its importance in securing a stable financial future. The chapter explains that compound interest/profit is the interest/profit earned on the principal amount invested and on the interest/profit earned over time. It is calculated based on the principal amount, the interest/profit rate, and the time period of the investment.

Besides that, the chapter highlights five critical factors to consider while calculating compound interest/profit: interest/profit rate, principal amount, frequency of compounding, duration, and deposits/withdrawals.

- The interest/profit rate is the rate at which you earn or pay interest, and it plays a significant role in determining the end result.
- The principal amount is the money you deposit or borrow, and it also affects the outcome of your investment. The frequency of compounding, whether daily, monthly, half-yearly, or yearly, affects the growth rate of your balance.
- The duration of holding the investment or debt also affects the growth rate, and the longer the investment is held, the more you will earn or owe.
- Finally, deposits or withdrawals affect the growth of your balance, and how quickly you pay off your debt or increase your principal sum can significantly affect your investment outcome.

By the end, the chapter encourages the younger generation to learn the magic of Compound interest/profit and shares a few pointers that tell,

1. Give Yourself Some Time
2. Pay Off Debts Quickly
3. Compare APYs
4. Check the Compounding Rate

The chapter ends with the author developing a rough strategic plan, urging the young generation that they can also become millionaires.

Chapter 7: Investing

"The biggest risk of all is not taking one."

-Mellody Hobson

Investing is about taking a risk. Trust me, there are no two ways about it. However, as a layperson trying to accumulate wealth, you would constantly fear losing your hard-earned money or making poor investment decisions. Nonetheless, as Robert Payne (a financial expert and economist) calls it, this constant fear of losing your investment can leave you vulnerable, which happens to be the biggest mistake one could ever make. He claims investing conservatively when you are young can leave you in a difficult position when you grow old. As suggested by economic professionals, the ideal age to consider high-risk investment is in your twenties and thirties. This is when you do not fear taking risks; you do not perceive risk concretely and are less likely to make any unsound decision.

But even if you are young, you can find the whole concept of investment mind-boggling. The reason is most of us are new to the world of investment. But in this world, we have nobody who can lay the foundation for us, so somehow, we end up violating the rules that usually go against us.

Given that, in this chapter, I will go through the rules

governing investment so that you do not flout any of its laws. Before that, let's look into the concept of investment from the very scratch.

What is an investment? Investment is an asset acquired or money committed with the purpose of earning income in the future. Investments are also made to benefit from future appreciation in the value of an asset. Investment is a purchase of future-oriented goods aimed at earning income in the future or creating wealth in the future. An individual may also seek to gain by selling the asset in the future for a higher price. This explains why a purchase without material value cannot be considered an investment. In addition to that, you should be wary of the fact that your investment should always generate income. If you own something valuable but it does not help you develop any income, I am sorry to tell you that it is not an investment. This is where most people end up creating the biggest blunder while considering investing options. They believe the investment is restricted by a value attached to any assets but fail to recognize its consequences. As a financial expert, I know investing can get risky at times. Where investment can help you generate a steady stream of income, it can also make you lose money, and you may lose your capital. Following safe guidelines can minimize the chances of losing your investment and maximize the opportunities to double it; how so? Here is what you can do to protect your capital.

Diversify Your Assets

I have never encountered any economic professional who does not promote the diversification of assets. It is a process in which you spread your investment to multiple sources to avoid potential risks.

Learning to balance your degree of comfort with risk and your time horizon is one of the keys to successful investment. If you invest your savings too cautiously when you're young, you'll likely fall prey to two of the widespread risks. Either your investments' growth rate won't keep up with inflation, or your investments might not increase to the level you need. On the other hand, if you invest too aggressively as you age, you can expose your savings to market volatility, which could devalue them.

To avoid such mishaps, investors prefer to spread their investments to multiple sources so that if one asset faces a loss, the other can generate profit in its stead. This is what diversification is all about. You put your investment separately while adding new money to it over a long period so that you can avoid the wrong timing. Speaking of which, diversification does not necessarily guarantee profit; however, it does lessen your chances of losing all the investment by not letting you keep all your eggs in one basket.

Don't forget, once you finish the saving part, you must consider all your options and see which one could benefit you the most. Here are some of the ways to carefully examine all your options.

Ways to Assess Your Investment

Before you look into any of your investment plans, consider a few things to avoid future constraints; for instance, when would you require the investment? Are you in a position where you could make a risky investment? Or what can maximum go wrong if you lose the entire capital? How badly would it affect your life? A person who is in haste to accumulate wealth would feel more inclined toward risky investment. This is because they know the riskier the acquisition, the greater the gain. And this is exactly what they seek.

When it comes to short-term funds, people usually end up investing in low-yielding securities. This is the most common mistake people commit. On the other hand, you shouldn't pick riskier assets either if you are goal is short-term. The reason is you might have to face loss when the time comes to sell the assets. After all, the value of investments fluctuates pretty quickly. You must learn to wait for the right time and then sell when the market is at its best and not when it hits rock bottom.

Should I be Investing in Bonds and Stocks?

Once you have decided to invest your money, you will be directed to choose one route out of these: 1) equity (also known as stocks or shares) and 2) debt (also known as bonds). Both things differ significantly from each other. With stocks, the ownership of a company is transferred to shareholders, and they are offered dividends as profits. On the other hand, bonds offer the ability to participate in lending to a company, but there will be no ownership. Instead, the bond buyer receives interest/profit and principal payments over time. Investing in a stock and bond can sometimes be an immense benefit, but that is not always the case, and a person should always keep the possibility open. Here's when your investment will make money:

- Investors should know that the company is good, so when it is the right time to sell their investment, others want to buy it.
- The company outperforms its rivals.

- The business is profitable, implying it has enough cash to pay you interest/profit on your bonds or even dividends on your stock.

There could be times when your investment will make no money at all.

- Customers are not interested in purchasing the company's goods or services.
- Company agents are unable to effectively manage the business, they overspend, and their expenses exceed their profits.
- Different financial backers who should sell accept that the organization's portions are too costly, given its future execution and possibilities.
- The rival business is superior to the company.
- They either fabricate false financial figures to deceive investors or claim that they have contracts to sell their products when they do not. Moreover, they argue profits from the past or the future that do not exist.
- The price of company stock is manipulated by brokers mostly. This is an attempt to hide the company's true value. These brokers sell the shares after the price goes up; the stock price goes down consequently, and investors lose money.
- When the market is going down, you have to sell your investment instantly.

People willing to invest in the market without considering these factors should look into it again. These pointers should not be neglected if you are serious about your goal.

Investment & Stock Market

First things first, the stock market deals with numerous shares from multiple organizations within a day. This means when an investor sells a share for any reason, another is purchasing and making a profit. This is why you should seriously consider your choice while investing your money in stocks.

What Causes Fluctuations in the Stock Market?

Like any other product in the market, the stock market also goes through some hinges occasionally. This majorly relies on supply and demand. When the number of shares available for purchase is insufficient to satisfy investor demand, prices rise; when fewer investors are interested in purchasing shares, they fall. However, considering a few of the elements, you can identify if the market will rise or fall. Situations like social and political unrest, natural disasters, opinions of famous investors, and media can heavily impact the stock market.

Best Time to Trade Stock

Europe entered World War II in 1939 after Germany invaded Poland. Fear and despair engulfed the entire world, paralyzing it. At that time, one of the greatest investors of all time, John Templeton, put $10,000 into the New York stock exchange. He purchased 100 shares of each company deemed to be on the verge of bankruptcy for less than $1.

Most people overlook the fact that bad circumstances won't last forever. Financial winter is a season followed by spring. Templeton became a multibillionaire as a result of the U.S. economy's boom following the end of the war in 1945. The ability to learn to invest while everyone else is fearful is what you have to master.

In 2009, the same thing transpired. But by the end of 2013, the market had grown by more than 142% from its low point. Yet, the majority of people squandered the chance. Why? Mostly due to human nature. We believe that once something is bad, it will never be better. Pessimism takes control.

Do you know that if you had invested in Amazon's stock ten years ago, that decision would have paid off majorly? A $1,000 investment in 2009 would be worth more than $13,300 as of December 9, 2019, for a total return of around 1,232%, according to CNBC calculations.

When to sell and when to acquire stock are the most important decisions that investors must make. The real-life example mentioned above demonstrates that it is best to buy when other people are pessimistic and sell when other people are actively optimistic. But keep in mind that when you buy, the chance of receiving a larger return is higher when the stock's price has decreased instead of when it has increased.

Therefore, it is advised to exercise caution at all times. For instance, consider a corporation whose stock dropped by 40% or more. Why did that happen? Are the stocks of other businesses in the same sector declining as well? Is the price drop significant? Is the stock market declining as a whole? If other companies in the same sector or industry, or stocks in the broader market, have been performing well, there may be an issue with the business you are considering investing in.

Active vs. Passive Investment Approach

Active investment is when a person assumes a portfolio manager role. It is based on a hands-on approach. The objectives of active money management are to beat the stock market's average returns and take full advantage of short-term price fluctuations. It necessitates a more in-depth analysis and the expertise to know when to pivot into or out of a specific stock, bond, or asset.

In contrast, the passive approach is about spreading your money to multiple companies. Investing in the passive approach would be a better choice for people interested in stocks.

In the active approach, the risk factor is usually high; it makes investors emotionally invested and suffer a great loss.

4 Major Classes of Assets

Asset classes are collections of investments with similar characteristics. A diversified portfolio should include a variety of asset classes to help balance risk.

The most common asset classes, sorted by risk and return, are as follows:

1. Cash and Equivalents

Many investors hold cash to preserve liquid assets or provide safety and comfort during volatile times; products resembling money, like treasury bills and commercial paper, are cash equivalents.

Return: Compared to other investments, cash and cash equivalents are thought to have a lower yield.

Risk: There's a little gamble concerning holding cash. The issuer's inability to repay the debt at maturity is a significant risk when investing in cash equivalents like commercial paper. Investors should think about the issuing company's characteristics, the business environment, and the economy before making a purchase.

2. Fixed Income or Bonds

Fixed income or bonds return the principal at a predetermined future date in exchange for fixed payments. Bonds are the most common type of fixed-income investment, but there are other types too. Certificates of deposit, for instance, are also regarded as fixed income.

Return: Fixed income assets refer to assets with a fixed yield. When you first invest, you can typically estimate your expected return, but you won't typically earn more than that.

Risk: There is a possibility that the government or business issuing the bond will not pay back the loan.

3. Real Assets

Buildings or oil barrels are tangible assets that make up real assets. Property and commodities are the most prevalent types of real assets. Investors may own offices, apartments, or industrial complexes to rent or sell for a profit.

Return: Real assets can appreciate in value. Additionally, investment properties can generate a substantial income, which can assist investors in combating inflation because rents frequently rise in line with the cost of living.

Risk: Real estate investments can be susceptible to risks associated with renting properties (such as rental defaults), changes in interest rates, fluctuations in the value of the underlying properties, and the impact of economic conditions on real estate values.

4. Commodities and Precious Metals:

Similar to real estate, commodities have material value too. It could be silver, gold, or oil. These things can be traded through future contracts and investing in an ETF.

Return: It tends to create a hedge against inflation since precious metals prices rise at or above the inflation rate.

Risk: The price of commodities and precious metals may constantly fluctuate.

ETFs and Index Fund

Learning investing basics includes understanding the difference between an index fund and an exchange-traded fund. An ETF is a pooled investment security. It functions similarly to a mutual fund. ETFs typically track a specific index, sector, commodity, or asset class; however, in contrast to mutual funds, ETFs can be purchased or sold on a stock exchange in the same manner as a regular stock.

An ETF can track anything from a small commodity's price to any securities. ETFs can even be designed to follow particular investment strategies. The major objective of EFT is to provide a portfolio to investors with a great range. Like stock prices, ETFs also fluctuate constantly throughout the day. However, they trade at a higher volume since they hold a group of stocks.

Whereas funds meant to replicate the performance and composition of a financial market index are known as index funds. They represent a hypothetical segment of the market. An index cannot be invested in by itself, but an index fund can. ETFs, like stocks, can be traded throughout the day, whereas index funds can be bought and sold only for the price set at the end of the trading day. Compared to purchasing an index fund, an ETF requires a minimum investment. So, for a beginner or even an experienced investor, ETFs seem like a great opportunity to invest in market indexes, like the S&P 500, at the lowest possible limit.

Index and exchange-traded funds (ETFs) are low-risk, low-maintenance, and low-cost ways to achieve long-term returns. However, these investments are not universal.

It would be best to consider which asset the fund follows and whether you prefer the fund's diversification or not when selecting an ETF or index fund. Then, compare the expense ratio of each fund and any other fees you might have to pay, like buying or selling commissions.

How to Pick Profitable ETFs

Here are four must-known criteria that should be critically followed when picking EFTs.

1. 5-year cumulative return must be greater than 50%
2. The expense ratio must be less than 0.20%
3. The distribution yield must be higher than 1.5%
4. The annual distribution must show an increasing trend consistently over the past three years.

5 Factors to Consider Before Investing

No matter where you choose to invest, it will always pose a certain level of risk to the capital. Most importantly, you take calculated risks and stick to a risk-to-reward ratio corresponding to your risk tolerance. Here are a few of the elements you should consider before you get into investment.

1. Build an Emergency Fund

Investing all your savings at once can throw you into some difficult positions. Instead, create a separate savings account to cover or pay for unexpected expenses. Life is highly unpredictable, and anything can happen to anyone at any time. However, keeping some amount on the side could prevent you from getting into a bigger problem. Indeed, saving provides a safety net and a way to achieve short-term goals.

2. Repay the High-Interest Debt

Paying all the remaining debt should be your first priority before investing. Especially when the interest rate on your debt is more than what you make. Getting rid of debt with high interest/profit rates is the best thing you can do for yourself.

3. Age Factor

When it comes to investing, age is a big factor. A person who has just started planning for retirement can experiment with stocks and other long-term investments, which would be too risky for someone who will soon retire. If you are closer to retirement age, you should consider options that pay dividends regularly. The older investors require greater security and have less time on their side; this is why they should rely less on the stock market while cash should be kept to a greater extent.

4. Budgeting for Investment

I have said this repeatedly: Creating a budget can do wonders for you, especially if you want to become an investor. It may seem daunting at first, but creating a simple budget with a spreadsheet will surely be helpful for you.

5. Compound Interest/Profit

In the previous chapter, I talked about compound interest/profit in great detail because I know nothing can compete against it. There is a reason why Einstein perceived compound interest as the eighth wonder of the world. A person who knows its importance can benefit significantly, but remember, an ignorant person who knows nothing about compounding will pay the price instead.

With over 20,000 mutual funds, individual stock, and bond offerings, going steady with your investment plan could be hard. Not to mention, if you have to win the race, you must go slow while preparing to kick any rising impediment that comes your way; as Warren Buffet says, *"The stock market is a device to transfer money from the impatient to the patient."*

Key Takeaways from This Chapter:

Chapter 7 of the book focuses on the means of investment and provides guidelines on how to protect your capital. The author defines investment as an asset acquired or money committed with the purpose of earning income in the future. It is also made to benefit from future appreciation in the value of an asset. It is important to note that an investment must always generate income. If an asset is valuable but does not help in developing any income, it cannot be considered an investment.

While making a risky investment, the author provides the following guidelines to protect the capital:

- Determine your investment goals
- Invest in a diversified portfolio
- Invest in low-cost index funds
- Avoid timing the market
- Seek advice from a financial expert

The chapter talks about the ways to assess investment, investing in bonds and stock, the causes that created fluctuation in the market, and the major classes of assets.

1. Cash and Equivalents
2. Fixed Income or Bonds
3. Real Assets
4. Commodities and Precious Metals
5. ETFs and Index Fund

The chapter concludes with the 5 factors to consider before investing, which include:

1. Build an Emergency Fund
2. Repay the High-Interest Debt
3. Age Factor
4. Budgeting for Investment
5. Compound Interest/Profit

Chapter 8: Investing in ETFs, Mutual Funds, and Bonds

"In investing, what is comfortable is rarely profitable."

-Robert Arnott

When it comes to investing, most people fear going against the grain. One possibility is they have become so entangled with their full-time jobs that they do not find enough time and energy to look into other ways of making money. But my concern is if people do not see the courage in the discomfort of investing, how would they ever break themselves free from modern-day slavery? As someone who has built everything from scratch, I can vouch that making a fortune and doing your 9-5 job can never go hand in hand.

Another reason, per my observation, is that some people get so comfortable with the road of mediocrity that looking for different ways to generate a good amount of income becomes a waste of time.

Certainly, deviating from your daily routine can cause you pain and discomfort, but this is a sign that you are moving forward in your life and should not fall back into your old pattern.

Given that, in this chapter, I will illuminate the best possible ways to accumulate wealth by considering multiple means of investment so that you don't have to rely on a small amount of your savings as a future security.

Ways to Build Wealth Through Investment

Believe it or not, when it comes to building wealth, you need to be focused more on diversification. Some people might consider putting all their eggs in one basket to avoid the hassle; however, if you want your wealth to last, you must allocate your investment to the appropriate assets. Here are some of the best ways for investors to build a diversified portfolio.

Exchange Traded Funds (ETFs)

For the investor who wants to diversify their investments while hedging the risk, this one is for you. Exchange-traded funds, also known as ETFs, are among the most common investment vehicles that permit investors to reap the maximum benefits with a low-cost portfolio. In simple words, ETFs are trade exchange stores where it is exchanged either on a trade or as stocks.

ETFs are eminent for replicating index holdings; consequently, they can monitor particular markets, geographic areas, or any other sector that an index can. They are generally considered passive investments since their objective is to track the performance of underlying investments.

On the other hand, actively managed funds like investment trusts strive to perform better than market return and, as a result, charge more to cover increased transaction costs and the expense of hiring a team of analysts.

ETFs are further classified into two categories: physical and synthetic ETFs. Similar to any other ETF, a synthetic ETF is directed to replicate the return of a specific index, such as the S&P 500 or the FTSE 100.

Besides that, synthetic ETFs use derivatives like swaps to track the underlying index. In addition to that, they prefer financial engineering over holding the underlying securities or assets to achieve the desired outcomes. Moreover, they can be bought or sold like usual shares, similar to traditional ETFs.

On the contrary, physical ETFs are responsible for holding most of the underlying securities that create a particular benchmark in the market. Here is an example of Betashares Australia 200 ETF owning all of the underlying securities of the Solactive Australia 200 Index to replicate its performance accurately.

Things to Consider Before Getting into ETFs

Though ETFs sound like an amazing idea, there is no harm in considering all the factors before you invest your hard-earned money.

1. Reputation of the ETF Provider

Before you get into ETFs, you must ensure every little detail about the provider. You might find it spooky, but trust me, the reputation of the provider and the amount you are going to get in return are interconnected, and you should be paying a great amount of attention to their track record and assets under their management.

2. Methodology of the Index

When investing in ETFs, it is crucial to understand the quality of exposure you will be provided. It would be best if you had a clear idea of the methodology of the index being used by ETFs. Also, working with ETF issuers who have already established a good reputation in the market for working with reputable index providers will work in your best interest.

3. Total Cost of Ownership

Set side by side the total cost of purchasing and holding ETFs to other products of a similar nature, and make sure to include management fees and transaction costs while doing so.

4. Tracking Errors

As someone about to invest a large sum in EFTs, it should be your priority to scrutinize how well the ETF provider has replicated the index's performance in the past.

Mutual Funds

Most investors usually feel inclined toward mutual funds since it is an affordable way to diversify their portfolio. But how do mutual funds work?

- Mutual funds provide a wide range of styles and investment strategies.
- Professional money managers run them, and they choose which securities (stocks, bonds, etc.) to buy and when they should be sold.
- All fund investments and any income they generate are available to you.

Through mutual funds, investors can co-purchase stocks or bonds by permitting them to pool their money together. In mutual funds, each share represents an investor's stake and earnings. They sell shares to investors, making their portfolio by holding the collections.

Why Do People Choose Mutual Funds?

Investors usually prefer investing through mutual funds since they provide the following features:

1. Liquidity

Investing in mutual funds means you can redeem your shares at any given time. The shares will follow the current net assets value (NAV), including the redemption fees.

2. Expert Management

Mutual funds are hassle-free. Your fund manager will do all the hard labor for you. The experts will select the securities, allocate assets, and monitor the funds. All you need to do is choose a manager with a good market reputation and track record, and you will be good to go.

3. Diversification

In mutual funds, the manager allocates your investment to stocks of businesses operating in a variety of sectors and industries so that you won't have to go through any major risk of any company's failure.

4. Low Cost

Unlike individual investors, mutual funds typically have lower transaction costs because they simultaneously buy and sell many securities. In addition, purchasing multiple funds units in bulk will give more economical rates than buying mutual funds in isolation.

Bonds

As you get closer to retirement age, and if your mode of investment remains bond, then it is very likely that your financial advisor will ask you to increase the proportion of bonds in your investment portfolio to ride out volatility and the risk of having your net worth destroyed by a market crash. But before you get into all the complex talk of bonds, you need to learn what exactly they are and how they function.

A bond is typically an investment in which you, as the investor, lend money to a borrower, expecting to receive interest-bearing repayment at the end of the term. This means that not only federal and state governments issue bonds, but private companies can also issue them. The good part about bonds is since they are a type of fixed-income investment, you know what you will get back before you even buy them. With that, bonds provide a stable cash flow and are proven to be less volatile than stocks.

How Does Bond Work?

By purchasing a bond, you are lending your money to the company or government that issued the bond, and now you are entitled to interest/profit payments since you landed them this money. Once the bond matures, you will receive interest/profit in addition to the principal or par value, which is the amount you paid for the bond. However, one thing about the bond market is that it is sensitive to interest rate fluctuations.

In contrast to stocks, the terms of a bond's contract, a legal document outlining its characteristics, can significantly impact its value. Since each bond issue is unique, you should be well-equipped with all the specific terminology on a bond before investing in it.

Classifying Bonds

Listed below are some of the bond types that will help you categorize bonds per your requirements.

1. Corporate Bonds

Corporate bonds are provided by businesses that first review the credibility of these bonds and then hand them over to the investors. High-yield bonds are the lowest-rated corporate bonds because of the higher interest rate they pay to cover their higher risk.

Bond markets often offer more favorable terms and lower interest/profit rates than bank loans, so companies issue bonds to raise funds for large-scale projects.

2. Government Bond

As its name suggests, a government bond is issued by the government. These bonds are used to raise funds for large projects like hospitals or infrastructure and are constantly listed on the debt market.

Vanilla bonds, variable bonds, CPI bonds, and zero-coupon bonds are examples of bonds that can be issued as government bonds. These bonds are low risk since the chances for the government to default on their principal are less. Yet, you still be wary of the country's credit history. The higher the credit rating, the more likely that the government will pay back its debt.

3. Mortgage Bond

In mortgage bonds, the pool of assets is used as a backup to cope with worst-case scenarios like bankruptcy. Here, the bondholders will receive the property as collateral if the issuer defaults on the bond.

4. Collateral Trust Bond

Bonds backed by financial assets like stocks or notes are known as collateral trust bonds. Collateral bonds secure their funding through the intelligible property and are considered secured bonds.

However, the investors need to realize that this security comes with a price, and they will have to compromise a little on the interest/profit rate when investing through a collateral bond.

Key Advantages of Investing in Bond

1. Predictable and Stable Income

One thing I like about investing in bonds is that it predicts your income from the get-go. Moreover, holding onto the bond until maturity means you can get a stable investment return. Bondholders receive monthly, quarterly, half-yearly, or annual interest/profit payments depending on the bond terms.

Especially when you are closer to retirement age, you can better predict how much money you will have in your later years. Remember, an investor with a long way to go until retirement has plenty of time to make up for losses caused by deflation in the stock market.

2. Lower Initial Investment

Investing in bonds does not require a hefty sum. You can start investing in bonds with a minimum amount of $1,000, which is the face value. This amount can be increased in multiple of face value if the investor desires to. With that, bonds do not have any limitations when it comes to maximum investment.

3. Portfolio Diversification

If you are looking for secure ways to diversify your portfolio while reducing the risk to a minimum, then you should consider investing in bonds. Due to their less volatile nature, they are regarded as a defensive asset class.

Financial experts highly suggest diversifying the portfolio with high-quality bonds that can help enhance the total return by counter-balancing the credit and interest/profit rate risk.

4. Risk-Reward Ratio

Traders and investors manage their capital and loss risk using the risk-reward ratio. The ratio helps determine a trade's expected return and risk. Anything greater than 1:3 is considered to be an acceptable risk-to-reward ratio. Bonds have always proven to have a favorable ratio. Bonds have a higher return than fixed deposits, while the risk is almost the same. Not to mention, it is much safer than equity, which has the same compound returns.

5. Better Returns

If you compare bonds to bank FDs (Fixed Deposits) or maybe some other investment instruments, you will see a clear distinction in the return rate of both modes of investment. Bonds are known to yield higher and positive returns, with a few bonds ranging from 7 to 14 percent. Additionally, the AAA-rated bonds provide annual returns in the range of 6-9 percent.

Long story short, bonds are an efficient way to get higher returns than equities, are safe as opposed to fixed deposits, and can be liquid at any time. On the other hand, if you look into mutual funds, their prices do not deviate from the value of the securities in the portfolio, which could sometimes happen in ETFs. Given that there are advantages to investing in all of these investment options, you should weigh all your choices before deciding where you should invest; however, to avoid getting into risk, the best idea would be to diversify your investment equally.

Key Takeaways from This Chapter:

Chapter 8 outlines some of the best ways for investors to build a diversified portfolio. The chapter emphasizes that putting all your eggs in one basket is not a viable strategy for long-term wealth creation. One of the best ways to diversify your investments is through Exchange Traded Funds (ETFs) and mutual funds, which allow investors to reap the maximum benefits with a low-cost portfolio.

ETFs are traded on an exchange like stocks, and they are known for replicating index holdings. This means they can track specific markets, geographic areas, or any other sector that an index can. The chapter also emphasizes the importance of understanding the risks involved in investing and the need for a long-term investment strategy. It advises investors to consider their risk tolerance, investment goals, and time horizon before investing in any asset class. Finally, the chapter highlights the need for investors to diversify their portfolios across different asset classes to reduce risks and maximize returns. It consists of a sort of guide that tells the readers about the factors to consider before getting into Efts.

1. The reputation of the ETF Provider
2. Methodology of the Index
3. Total Cost of Ownership
4. Tracking Errors

As the chapter proceeds, the readers get introduced to mutual funds and why they should invest in them. Some of these reasons are:

1. Liquidity
2. Expert Management
3. Diversification
4. Low Cost
5. Bond

Lastly, the chapter discusses the key advantages of investing in bonds.

1. Predictable and Stable Income
2. Lower Initial Investement
3. Portfolio Diversification
4. Risk-Reward Ratio
5. Better Returns

Chapter 9: Entrepreneurship

"Any time is a good time to start a company."

-Ron Conway

Starting a new business can be daunting since it involves a great deal of uncertainty. Subsequently, being an entrepreneur means juggling countless things at a time while dedicating all your time and energy to it. Obviously, starting anything from scratch can never be easy. Trust me, you will have to give all your undivided attention to the business you just created while standing firm in the face of any challenge. That's exactly how you get to reap the fruit of your hard work, and there are no two ways.

Throughout my long-standing career, I have heard people approaching the idea of entrepreneurship with presuppositions like entrepreneurs are bound to fail. Let me be precise. Entrepreneurs do not fail because of their businesses; their companies die when they lose interest and fail when they cannot embrace failure.

I do not deny that the road to entrepreneurship is not littered with diversions and potholes. I have been there myself, and I know maintaining high passion and inventiveness while negotiating these obstacles can be challenging. These potholes can make you feel frustrated, and, at times, the stagnant growth of the business can make you feel like giving up too. But here is the reassurance: every entrepreneur goes through this phase at least once in their career. From Bezos to Jobs, all have been a part of this interim at one point in their lives, but their dedication to their business separates them from any ordinary person. They didn't give up on their goals because of some unexpected detour; instead, they bounced back with a bigger proposal even when their business hit rock bottom.

Here are some real-life accounts of prominent entrepreneurs who lost money but rebounded stronger after reaching the lowest possible point in their lives.

1. Thomas Edison

You might have heard about Thomas Edison's invention, but do you know that he marketed his product and turned it into a full-fledged business? Well, here is a brief account of Edison. He was deemed too stupid to learn anything during his early life, which continued to his workplace. Though with almost no help from any external source, Edison came up with a life-changing invention.

However, if you pay attention to this story, you will know that Edison's first try was an absolute disaster. He did not invent the light bulb overnight as many of us think; instead, he had to make countless attempts before finally creating it.

2. Walt Disney

To this date, Disney holds a great reputation among marketers and audiences. Walt Disney started his career as a commercial artist. He took over the world of animation along with his brother Roy and started working on their dream from a small studio in California. Though most of us only focused on his success story, Walt Disney never dismissed the reports of his struggling days. He proudly embraced his failures and setbacks like a true entrepreneur. He has always been vocal about his experiences and shared how he had to survive on dog biscuits until before the release of Mickey Mouse took over the animation industry. Apparently, it feels like Disney had everything sorted since day one, but is it really the case?

Walt Disney was constantly surrounded by financial difficulties, creative struggles, and even a bitter strike by his animators in 1941.

However, with his relentless pursuit of innovation and creativity, he made Disney what it is today. As an entrepreneur, he constantly pushed the boundaries of what was possible in animation and was unafraid to take risks and try new things.

3. Steve Jobs

Steve Jobs had a vision of creating products that were not just functional but also aesthetically pleasing, and he was able to create a company culture that shared his passion for design and innovation. Despite his many successes, he also experienced some notable failures in his life.

One of the most significant failures was the Apple Lisa computer, launched in 1983. The Lisa was a commercial failure due to its high price and poor performance, ultimately leading to Jobs' departure from the company. However, Jobs did not allow this setback to get into his head; instead, he took it as an opportunity to learn and establish his own business, and so today, the iPhone remains the most popular mobile device in the world.

Jobs' entrepreneurial journey was characterized by his willingness to take risks and pursue his vision, even in the face of failure. He was a master of branding and marketing and had a unique ability to anticipate and capitalize on emerging trends.

4. Henry Ford

"Failure is simply the opportunity to begin again, this time more intelligently." You must have heard this brilliant quote before, but do you know Henry Ford came up with these words of wisdom?

Henry Ford, widely regarded as the father of automobiles, is prominently known for bringing a sudden shift in how cars were manufactured.

Even though Ford's business reached the highest level of success, his tale of entrepreneurship faced several failures throughout his career. One of the most notable was the Ford Edsel, a car introduced in 1958, which was a commercial failure due to its high price and poor performance. Nonetheless, Ford did not heed the setback and continued his dedication to the cars.

All the aforementioned entrepreneurs were as ordinary as a common person, but they took a start from somewhere. They weren't scared of taking risks. Every time they hit rock bottom, they bounced back but never lost hope. Certainly, entrepreneurship is about taking the challenge and overcoming obstacles, but in my opinion, entrepreneurship is a highly rewarding and potentially lucrative investment. It is the first step toward expanding your investment.

As I said before, entrepreneurship may require a lot of time, patience, and a good amount of money, but it also has a massive potential return.

Here's a step-by-step guide on how to become an entrepreneur:

1) Identify Your Passion and Align It with Potential Markets

A strong passion for their work often drives successful entrepreneurs.

Certainly, having a profitable idea is significant for the product, but you should link your passion to market trends as well. This will prevent you from leaving your business hanging during tough times.

Consider your skills and interests and try to align your passion with what is in demand and marketable. Identify potential markets by figuring out what products and services are in high demand. Brainstorm ideas for how you can offer something unique and valuable to the market. Consider what trends are emerging and how you can capitalize on them. Think about what you can do to differentiate your business from the competition.

2) Research the Market

Once you have identified a business idea to pursue, research the market and potential customers to test the waters. Market research gives you vital knowledge about the industry and its competitive environment. It informs you of how the target clients and customers may view your business. Moreover, it introduces you to the existing big players within the industry, their current standing in the market, and their competitive advantages. Having a profound knowledge of all this would help you differentiate your offering from theirs.

Why is this crucial?

Market research provides aid in your understanding of how to interact with your potential competitors and guides the planning of your subsequent actions. You should conduct market research right after identifying your passions and before drafting the idea for your business to understand your target audience, competitors, and industry trends. This will help you develop a viable business plan and ensure demand for your product or service.

3) Develop a Business Plan

Developing a business plan for an entrepreneur is a strategic tool and should be taken seriously. As Benjamin Franklin once said, *"If you fail to plan, you are planning to fail."* Before you get into all the technicalities, you need to create a plan to help you succeed and distinguish your short-term and long-term goals.

Entrepreneurs seeking funds from institutional investors and lenders should create a valuable business plan that should speak for itself.

Based on your passion and market research, develop a business idea that aligns with your goals and values. Think about what problem you are solving or what value you are offering. Your business plan should include a description of your product or service, market analysis, marketing and sales strategies, and financial projections.

4) Build Your Team

Building a cohesive team that works towards a single objective requires great exertion, but it is necessary. A close-knit team guarantees productivity and collaboration. The significance and primary goal of team building is to forge links and connections that will help the team become strong.

Successful entrepreneurs surround themselves with a team of skilled professionals who can help them to achieve their goals. Hire people who share your vision and have the necessary skills and experience. Your team may include employees, advisors, mentors, and partners.

5) Secure Funding

Next, you need to assess your resources. As someone starting a business, you should be able to audit your assets and liability, and as a rule of thumb, you should only invest the amount you can afford to lose. You should be aware of your financial standing and have a clear and concise idea of what amount should be kept for investment. You can also perform a break-even analysis to determine the amount required for the investment purpose.

Here is how you can calculate it:

$$\text{Fixed Costs} \div (\text{Average Price} - \text{Variable Costs})$$

Your next step should be determining how much money you need to start your business and exploring funding options, such as loans, grants, and investments.

Develop a financial analysis that outlines your expenses and revenue projections. Be prepared to present your business plan and financial prediction to potential investors.

6) Register with Tax Authorities (If Required)

If you plan to start a business as an entrepreneur, you must register with the relevant tax authorities (if any) to obtain a tax identification number. This number, also known as an Employer Identification Number (EIN), is used to identify your business entity for tax purposes. To register your business with the tax authorities and obtain an EIN, you need to:

- Determine the type of business entity you have. Several types of business entities exist in the market, including

sole proprietorship, partnership, corporation, and Limited Liability Company (LLC).
- You will need to decide on some particulars of your business, such as the legal name or the mailing address.
- You may apply for an EIN online by mail, fax, or phone. The quickest and easiest way to obtain an EIN is through the online application on the website.
- Once you have your EIN, you must understand your tax obligations as a business entity.

7) Launch Your Business

Once you have secured funding and built your team, launching your business is the next step. Develop a timeline for launching your business because the final step requires you to do many necessary things. For instance, developing a website, creating marketing materials, and investing in branding and customer service to attract and retain customers.

Don't forget to develop a plan for long-term growth and expansion. Ensure you stay abreast with the market trends and remain prepared to adapt and make changes as you learn from your customers and their feedback.

Why Should You Become an Entrepreneur?

Being an entrepreneur means you will have to walk on difficult paths while working for more than the required hours.

As quoted by Shark Tank, an American business reality television series, "Entrepreneurs are the only people who will work 80 hours a week to avoid working 40 hours a week." Well, where this might seem funny, it is actually the reality. Entrepreneurs work day and night to see their dreams come true and to make sure their plans come to fruition, but they dedicate themselves to their work because they enjoy doing it. Being an entrepreneur means you will get to witness the pros that are attached to it.

Here are some of the key benefits of being an entrepreneur that you should know:

1. Financial Rewards

One of the most appealing benefits of entrepreneurship is the potential for financial rewards. Successful entrepreneurs can earn substantial profits and can accumulate wealth over time. Moreover, being an entrepreneur means you get to decide your own income rather than your income being chosen by some hiring manager. Aside from the high risk of entrepreneurship, it also has the potential for massive rewards.

2. Control and Flexibility

The good part about being an entrepreneur is that you do not have to deal with any authority above you; you are the authority, i.e., your own boss. You have the ability to control and make your destiny. You are now in charge of your schedule. You do not have to rely on anyone to make decisions and can work on projects that interest you.

Tell me, what could be better than that?

3. Innovation and Creativity

Entrepreneurship is for people who are open to changes and prefer risk-taking. Unlike commoners who fear trying new things, they have the right mind for experiments.

Entrepreneurs have complete liberty over their innovation and believe in going beyond their creativity to pursue new ideas and opportunities. They are not bound to restrict their creativity while developing new products and services that can impact the world.

4. Personal Growth

Starting and running a business can be challenging, but it can also be a rewarding personal growth experience. You can develop new skills and gain valuable experience in areas such as leadership, problem-solving, and decision-making.

5. Community Impact

Entrepreneurs can positively impact their communities by creating jobs and driving economic growth. They can also make a difference by supporting local causes and charities.

To sum it up, entrepreneurship plays a crucial role in growth and development. It drives innovation, creates job opportunities, and fosters economic growth. Furthermore, entrepreneurship allows individuals to turn their passions and ideas into reality while positively impacting the world.

If you have a vision, passion, and desire to make a difference, entrepreneurship is the right career path for you. You can be your own boss, set your own goals and priorities, and directly impact your business' success. However, bear in mind that entrepreneurship may seem like it's a direct road that leads to wealth, but it is not for everyone and requires a great deal of hard work, dedication, and resilience.

Remember, becoming an entrepreneur is a journey that demands perseverance and a willingness to take risks. But with a strong passion, a solid business plan, and a great team, you can achieve your goals, build a successful business the way you want, and enjoy the wealth you will get to accumulate!

Key Takeaways from This Chapter:

In Chapter 9, the author discusses common misconceptions about entrepreneurship and highlights the importance of perseverance and embracing failure. The author notes that entrepreneurs do not fail because of their businesses but rather because they lose interest or fail to adapt to challenges. The chapter encourages the readers to stay committed to their goals and maintain their passion for their business. With that, it provides a step-by-step guide on how to become an entrepreneur:

- Identify Your Passion and Align It with Potential Markets
- Research the Market
- Develop a Business Plan
- Build Your Team
- Secure Funding
- Register with Tax Authorities
- Launch Your Business

In closing, the chapter urges the readers to discover why they want to become entrepreneurs, and with that, the author has come up with his reason that would support the chapter from beginning to end. These reasons include financial rewards, control and flexibility, innovation and creativity, personal growth, and community impact.

Chapter 10: Currency and Commodities Trading

"The goal of a successful trader is to make the best trades. Money is secondary."

-Alexander Elder

Now that I have given a detailed account of trading and investment in the previous chapters, I believe it is the right time to explore some less-chosen ways of trading that are worth giving a shot at. But before we find ourselves completely submerged in the topic, let's look into the core of currency and commodities training and see how it works.

First things first, what are currency and commodities trading?

Currency trading, commonly known as *'forex'* (foreign exchange), is a process of buying and selling currencies to generate a profitable return. The foreign exchange market is the world's largest and most liquid financial market, with an estimated daily turnover of over $5 trillion. Unlike the stock market, where investors buy and sell shares of companies, currency trading involves the exchange of one currency for another at an agreed-upon price.

On the other hand, commodities trading is the buying and

selling of physical goods, such as precious metals, oil, agricultural products, and other natural resources. This market is essential to the global economy, allowing producers and consumers to hedge against price fluctuations and manage risk.

Distinction Between Commodities and Forex

There is no lie that commodities and forex trading are highly favored by investors, along with the equity market; however, before you choose any of these as your trading mode, I would suggest building a clear knowledge of the different instruments and strategies involved in the different types of trading. Keeping this in mind, I have come up with some key distinctions between forex and commodities trading.

1. The Appropriate Market for Trading

One of the biggest differences between currency and commodities trading stems from the market where the trade is being made. Believe it or not, knowing about your goals and aligning them with the market can save you from potential risk. As Warren Buffet says, *"I make no attempt to forecast the market—my efforts are devoted to finding undervalued securities."* That said, you should learn to differentiate between the market for commodities and forex trading to know which option would work in your best interest.

As far as currency trading is concerned, it takes place in the foreign exchange market (also known as *'forex'*). On the contrary, commodities trading does not occur in a single market and can be found in various commodity markets (such as energy, precious metals, agriculture, etc.).

2. Instruments Involved in the Trading

When it comes to currency trading, traders buy and sell currency pairs, while in commodities trading, traders buy and sell commodities such as gold, oil, wheat, etc.

3. Exchange Rate Volatility

Currency trading tends to be more volatile than commodities trading, as exchange rates fluctuate rapidly due to various economic and political factors. On the other hand, commodity prices can also be affected by supply and demand factors but tend to be more stable over the long term.

3. Trading with Leverage

Currency trading often involves higher leverage than commodities trading. Simply put, this gives traders enough control over larger positions with smaller amounts of capital. This could be great for generating potential returns, but at the same time, it can make the traders deal with potential risks.

4. Trading Strategies

Currency trading generally includes short-term trading strategies, like day trading and scalping. On the other hand, commodities trading often involves longer-term strategies, which include trend following and position trading.

5. Market Participants

If we look into currency trading, it is dominated by institutional investors such as banks, hedge funds, and central banks. As opposed to commodities trading, which has a wider range of participants, including producers, traders, and speculators.

Not to mention, both currency and commodities trading can be profitable, but they require different skills, knowledge, and strategies. It should be the prime duty of a trader to carefully consider their goals, risk tolerance, and experience before choosing which market to trade in.

Opting for Commodities Trading

As I said earlier, commodities and forex trading are getting on the good side of investors owing to their diversification, transparency, market, low trading cost, etc.

To better understand forex and commodities trading, let's look into their benefits separately.

Pros of Commodities Trading

- Commodities trading provides a good deal of diversification benefits to a portfolio since they have a low correlation with other asset classes, such as stocks and bonds.
- Commodities, such as precious metals, energy, and agricultural products, can act as a barrier against inflation since their prices tend to rise during periods of inflation.
- Commodities trading typically requires a lower margin than other asset classes, making it accessible to traders with smaller accounts.
- Commodities markets are highly transparent, with price information and market news readily available to traders.
- Commodities markets are global, and traders can access them 24 hours a day, providing ample trading opportunities.

Pros of Forex Trading

- The forex market is the most liquid in the world, with daily trading volume exceeding $6 trillion, providing traders ample trading opportunities.
- Forex trading allows traders to trade with leverage. As mentioned before, it enables investors to get the hang of larger positions with smaller capital investments.

- Like the commodity market, the forex trade also remains operational 24 hours a day, five days a week, allowing traders to participate at any time.
- Forex trading typically has lower trading costs than other markets, making it an affordable option for traders.
- Forex trading is a global market, providing traders with access to a wide range of currency pairs and trading opportunities worldwide.

Since we have covered the basics of commodities and currency trading already, at this point, we cannot afford to neglect currency pairs and their distinct types.

Knowing Currency Pair

So far, I have mentioned this term a few times, and I am sure it must have created confusion among the readers since the term is relatively new to them. To make things clear, here is a clear and concise explanation of currency pairs and on what grounds they are being categorized.

A currency pair comprises two different currencies which are traded in the foreign exchange market. The value of a currency pair is determined by the exchange rate between the two currencies. For example, the EUR/USD currency pair represents the Euro and US dollar exchange rate. The first currency in the pair is called the base currency, and the second is called the quote currency. Currency pairs are traded in the forex market, which is the largest financial market in the world.

There are three main categories of currency pairs: major, minor, and exotic.

- Major currency pairs are the most frequently traded pairs and include the EUR/USD, GBP/USD, and USD/JPY pairs.
- Minor currency pairs include less frequently traded pairs such as the NZD/CAD and the CHF/JPY.
- Exotic currency pairs involve a major currency paired with a currency from an emerging or less developed economy, such as the USD/MXN or the EUR/TRY pairs.

Short Selling and Options Trading

Before you take a plunge in short selling or options trading, getting acquainted with the two markets briefly would be great. Here's a brief account of short selling and options trading, respectively.

For starters, short selling is a strategy traders use to seek profit from a decline in the price of an asset. The concept of short selling is simple to comprehend. An investor borrows an asset, usually a stock or a commodity, from a broker and immediately sells it at the current market price. The investor hopes that the asset's price will fall in the future, allowing them to buy it back at a lower price and return it to the broker, thus making a profit from the difference.

Short selling is most commonly used in the stock market but can also be applied to other assets, such as commodities or currencies.

Moving on to options trading, an investment strategy in which an investor buys and sells options contracts on a specific underlying asset, such as commodities or currencies.

Options trading is a popular way for investors to keep the risk at bay, generate income, or speculate on the direction of an asset's price movement.

Options trading is further divided into two major categories.

1. Call Options

Call options give the holder the right to buy the underlying asset at a specific price, i.e., they act as a contract between the buyer and the seller to purchase stock until a defined expiration. Investors and traders often use them to speculate on an underlying asset's future price movements or predict against potential losses. When a call option is exercised, the buyer pays the strike price and receives the underlying asset from the seller.

2. Put Options

Put options give the holder the right to sell the underlying asset at a specific price. Options traders can use various strategies to profit from the market, including buying and selling options outright and using more complex strategies such as spreads and straddles.

Getting Started with Commodities and Forex Trading

Currency and commodities trading can be a little challenging for some traders. This could be because most people are unfamiliar with its benefits, consisting of unique challenges, unlike equity. However, trading commodities and currencies can greatly diversify your portfolio and potentially earn profits.

Here are some general tips on how to kick-start your trading career in these markets:

1. Broaden Your Knowledge

Before you get into trading, it should be your priority to understand the fundamentals of the commodity or currency you're interested in trading. This could include factors like supply and demand, geopolitical events that could affect prices, and economic indicators that could signal shifts in the market.

2. Look for a Mediator

If you have already planned to get into commodities and currency trading, you need to start looking for a broker as soon as possible. Working with a broker will allow you to access the commodities and currencies markets easily.

Make sure you look for a reputable broker that offers low fees, access to the markets you're interested in, and educational resources to help you make informed decisions.

3. Develop a Trading Strategy

After you have found a broker, your next step should be developing a solid strategy that should be able to tick all the required boxes.

Remember that your trading strategy should consider a few of the significant elements, including your risk tolerance, investment goals, and market analysis. This may include using technical analysis to identify entry and exit points or fundamental analysis to anticipate market shifts.

4. Practice with a Demo Account

As far as trading is concerned, it is something that cannot be taken lightly. Your money is on it, and I am sure you would not want to lose a single penny just because you were not well-equipped with the tools or instruments. Lukman Otunuga, a financial expert, claims that trading is a serious activity and should be considered as one. He further argues that traders should see the significance of a demo account so that they can learn about the key indicators beforehand.

The good part is many brokers offer demo accounts that allow you to practice trading with virtual funds before you risk real money. This tool can be valuable for testing your trading strategy and getting comfortable with the platform.

5. Monitor the Markets

Understanding and monitoring the market should be a must for all traders since it will greatly help in forecasting when the market goes up or hits rock bottom.

Stay up-to-date with news and events that could affect your trading commodity or currency. This could include following social media accounts, subscribing to newsletters, or setting up alerts on your trading platform.

6. Manage Your Risk

Trading commodities and currencies carry a significant amount of risk with them. Given that, it's important to have a risk management strategy in place. This could include setting stop-loss orders to limit potential losses or diversifying your portfolio to spread risk across multiple assets.

7. Keep Records

Lastly, do not forget to keep a detailed record of your trades. It should consist of entry and exit points, profits or losses, and any notes regarding your strategy.

Recording your strategy can help you analyze your performance over time and will allow you to make adjustments to your strategy as per the need.

In essence, commodity and currency exchange are important components of the global financial system. Commodity trading allows producers and consumers of raw materials to manage price risks and ensure stable supplies of essential goods.

Meanwhile, currency exchange markets enable individuals and businesses to exchange one currency for another, facilitating international trade and investment.

Key Takeaways from This Chapter:

Chapter 10 of the book explores some alternative ways of trading that are worth considering beyond traditional methods. However, before delving into the topic, the chapter provides an overview of currency and commodities trading, two significant financial market aspects. It also provides a detailed comparison between commodities and forex trading. The chapter further highlights the first key difference between the two markets, which is the appropriate market for trading. It provides valuable advice for traders interested in currency and commodities trading.

To kick-start a trading career in these markets, the author provides seven tips.

- Firstly, traders should prioritize understanding the fundamentals of the commodity or currency they plan to trade.
- Secondly, they should find a reputable broker.
- Thirdly, traders need to develop a solid trading strategy that considers their risk tolerance, investment goals, and market analysis.
- Fourthly, the author recommends practicing with a demo account
- Fifthly, traders should monitor the markets closely.
- Sixthly, traders must have a risk management strategy
- Lastly, traders should keep a detailed record of their trade.

Chapter 11: Investment in Real Estate

"Ninety percent of all millionaires become so through owning real estate."

-Andrew Carnegie

So far, I have discussed multiple lucrative ways of investment in the previous chapters, and I assure you, they are pretty legible for all of my readers. Bearing this in mind, I have decided to elevate the game by going ahead with our investment goal. So here, in this chapter, I will introduce a high-remunerative mode of investment that will help you grow your wealth steadily and safely.

Having said that, what is the first thing that comes to your mind when somebody talks about investment? Investing in stock? Investing in commodities? For most people, investment is directly linked to selling and purchasing properties. But you know what baffles me? Even when real estate property is the first thing that comes to mind, people are still not quite aware of the appropriate ways to invest in real estate, and they usually fall prey to the inherent danger. As I have said before, you don't have to fear a thing because this book includes all the potential risks and their antidote so that you stay prepared to fight the potential danger. Not to mention, real estate investment is among the best vehicles to grow wealth if you are willing to learn every necessary detail.

So, let's quickly get into it without prattling anymore.

What Is Real Estate Investment?

To begin with, let's look into the basics of real estate investment.

Real estate investment is a lucrative way to earn passive income, build wealth, and diversify your portfolio since it involves purchasing, owning, managing, renting, or selling property to generate a profit. The real estate market is a vast and dynamic industry that includes residential, commercial, and industrial properties. However, each sector has its own unique set of challenges, risks, and potential rewards.

This being said, the power of real estate investment turned 90% of commoners into millionaires, but there is more to it. These people became successful real estate investors because they understood the importance of thorough research, due diligence, and strategic planning when investing in properties. The same goes for you.

Even if you are a seasoned investor or a newbie, you need to understand the fundamentals of real estate investment to accumulate wealth while you sleep, and what could be a better way to invest your money if not in the land?

As John Stuart Mills, an English philosopher, said, *"Landlords grow rich in their sleep without working."*

There is no better way to accumulate a steady income and secure your financial future than real estate investment. With the potential for stable rental income, tax benefits, and property appreciation, real estate can be a powerful tool for achieving financial goals.

However, here is a disclaimer. All my readers should approach real estate investment with cautious planning. Bear in mind real estate investment is not only about owning random property but also about understanding market trends, identifying profitable opportunities, and managing risk. Together, they all play a crucial role in successful real estate investment.

The Basics of Investing In Real Estate

Believe it or not, real estate investment can be an outstanding addition to your portfolio. It will help you enhance your investment while allowing you to generate a tax-free passive income. It is an act of buying, managing, and selling or renting real estate properties to generate a profit. This involves various tasks, including property selection, financial analysis, property management, and marketing.

In the real estate investment world, investors must be knowledgeable about the market, have access to financing, and possess management and negotiation skills.

Here is a step-by-step guide that will aid you in understanding real estate and how it works.

Selecting the Right Property

The first step in real estate investment is selecting the right property. Investors must consider multiple factors, including location, property condition, and market trends.

The trick is to find a property that is undervalued or has the potential to generate a high return on investment. Once you have selected the property, the investor needs to perform a financial analysis to determine whether the investment is viable. This includes evaluating the potential cash flow, return on investment, and risk associated with the investment.

Managing/Maintaining the Property Effectively

After acquiring the property, the next step should be maintenance with regard to profit-maximizing. Property management is a critical aspect of real estate investment and can significantly impact the profitability of the investment.

The investor needs to manage the concerned property effectively to generate a good amount of profit. This involves various tasks, including property maintenance, dealing with tenants, and financial management. The goal is to keep the property in good condition, attract and retain tenants, and maximize rental income.

To Sell the Property or Rent It Out?

You, as an investor, can decide whether to sell or rent a well-maintained and managed property by aligning your personal goals with your financial plan. Selling the property could be the right choice if the property has good value. Furthermore, it can generate a high return on investment if it has appreciated in value. In contrast, renting the property can provide a steady income stream over an extended period.

Not to mention, the decision to sell or rent the property depends on multiple factors, including market conditions, financial goals, and personal preferences.

Key Reasons to Invest in Real Estate

There are several compelling reasons why investing in real estate can be an intelligent financial decision.

1. Potential for High Returns

Most people fear the volatile nature of the investment, precisely crypto and forex, which is understandable. But people looking for safe ways to invest their savings in such a way that inflation should not affect them should definitely opt for real estate investment for three reasons.

1. Real estate investment can offer high returns on investment, particularly compared to other investment options. Property appreciation and tax benefits all contribute to significant returns over time.
2. Real estate investments can generate consistent rental income, providing a steady stream of passive income that can be reinvested or used to supplement other sources of income.
3. Real estate investors can use borrowed funds to finance the purchase of a property and can increase the potential returns on investment. This implies that investors are using less of their own money to purchase a property and can benefit from the potential for property appreciation and rental income.

2. Diversification

Real estate investment can effectively diversify your investment portfolio, spreading out risk and reducing volatility. This can be particularly important for those who are heavily invested in other assets, such as stocks and bonds. Investing in real estate is generally seen as a conservative investment strategy since land value stays unaffected even when the market falters.

3. Cash Flow

One of the significant benefits of real estate investment is the potential for consistent cash flow. Rental income can provide a steady stream of passive income that can be reinvested or used to supplement your other sources of income.

4. Hedge Against Inflation

It is not a hidden secret that rental values increase over time in line with inflation. Given that, real estate can generally serve as a hedge against inflation. This can help protect your wealth and purchasing power over the long term.

5. Tangible Asset

The land you own, the house in which you live, and the studio you purchased will always have a value attached to them. Your investment through currency might dip to zero, or the stock market will falter, but the land will protect you from hitting rock bottom. In addition, unlike other investment options, real estate is a tangible asset that can be seen and touched, providing a sense of security and stability that is not always present with other investments.

As a matter of fact, real estate investment offers a range of benefits for investors, ranging from high returns and consistent cash flow to diversification and tax benefits.

Ten Smart Real Estate Investment Tips

As a financial expert, I refuse to see real estate investment as entirely profitable. Yes, it requires risk management and is prone to currency fluctuations, but my point is that investing in real estate is comparatively less risky and offers several benefits that make it an attractive investment option for many people. Investing in real estate can be a rewarding investment strategy, but it's crucial to approach it carefully and with a clear plan.

Here are ten valuable secret tips that most successful investors are gate-keeping from you.

1. Know Your Goal

First things first, before you get into real estate investment, it's essential to define your investment goal.

Ask yourself, what exactly do you want? Do you want to generate income from rental properties, flip properties for a profit, or hold onto properties for long-term appreciation? This might not seem very important, but coming from experience, understanding your goals can help guide your investment strategy.

2. Learning About the Market

Deciding a goal is essential, but at the same time, you need to have a good grip on the real estate market to not miss out on a potential opportunity. Learning about the real estate market is no rocket science and is easier than you could think.

All you need to do is research the local real estate market to gain insight into property values and trends. This is an efficient way to identify investment opportunities, and the acquired knowledge will help you make informed decisions about which properties are worth investing in.

3. Time to Set a Budget

As someone newly joining the real estate market, you might not have considered setting a clear budget at the moment. Well, you are not alone in this. I would rather call it the most common blunder that investors make. They usually don't plan a budget because they have no time for it, but in the end, they are the ones who end up getting entangled in multiple headaches.

Create a budget by determining how much you can afford to invest in real estate, considering your financial situation, financing options, and potential income from the property.

4. Your Location Matters

Getting into real estate investment without knowing how to assess the value of land will get you nowhere. Location is critical in real estate investing, as properties in desirable locations tend to appreciate in value and attract renters. Houses with little expansion room are usually desirable to those with plenty of space. Look for properties in areas with strong economic growth, good schools, and access to transportation. When investing in real estate, from zoning laws to demographics, everything plays a key role.

5. Analyze Potential Properties

Once you have identified your desired property, analyze it carefully to determine its potential for profitability. Consider other factors, including purchase price, rental income, operating expenses, and potential appreciation.

6. Secure Financing

When it comes to real estate investing, you need to be very precise about your finances. Real estate investments often require significant capital, so it's essential to secure financing before making a bid on a property. Get into the market and explore options such as traditional mortgages, private loans, or partnerships with other investors.

7. Hire a Team of Professionals

Being new in the market means you are more likely to commit mistakes since real estate investing can get complex. Working with a team of professionals, such as real estate agents, attorneys, and accountants, can help you navigate the process smoothly.

8. Invest in Property Improvements

Investing in property improvements, such as renovations or upgrades, can help increase the property's value and attract higher-quality renters.

9. Monitor Market Trends/Property Cycle

Keep an eye on market trends and measure the property cycle from time to time. This will aid you in adjusting your investment strategy accordingly. For instance, if rental rates in your area are rising, you may want to consider investing in rental properties.

10. Be Patient

The first and foremost rule of any investment is to be patient, and if I talk about real estate investment, it is a long-term strategy that demands time and patience. While investing in real estate, being patient and taking a strategic approach are essential. Don't rush into investments without proper research and analysis, and be prepared to hold onto properties for several years to maximize their potential for appreciation.

If you follow these tips and develop a clear investment plan, you can maximize the potential benefits of real estate investing and build a profitable portfolio of properties over time.

In essence, real estate investment can be a profitable and rewarding venture for those willing to put in the time, effort, and capital. With proper due diligence and sound strategy, real estate can be a lucrative investment opportunity for both experienced and novice investors.

Key Takeaways from This Chapter:

Chapter 11 discusses the fundamentals of real estate investment, starting from the various types of real estate properties to the critical factors that need to be considered before making any investment decisions. The chapter provides a step-by-step guide on how to invest in real estate effectively.

- The first step in real estate investment is selecting the right property.
- Property management is a critical aspect of real estate investment and can significantly impact the profitability of the investment.
- The decision to sell or rent the property depends on multiple factors, including market conditions, financial goals, and personal preferences.
- Investors in real estate must be knowledgeable about the market, have access to financing, and possess management and negotiation skills.
- It highlights the importance of location when investing in real estate.

Additionally, this chapter highlights ten-smart real estate investment tips.

- The first rule is to know your goal
- Understand the market
- Set a budget
- Your location matters
- Analyze potential properties

- Secure financing
- Hire a team of professional
- Invest in property improvement
- Monitor property cycle
- Be patient

Chapter 12: Diversifying Your Investment Portfolio

"Diversify. In stocks and bonds, as in much else, there is safety in numbers."

-Sir John Templeton

A very common maxim says, *"Don't put all your eggs in one basket."* The same adage goes well when applied to stocks and investments. Putting all your eggs in one basket makes you more susceptible to a substantial loss since all your investments are in one place. That's one reason most financial experts suggest diversifying the portfolio for better outcomes. As a matter of fact, there is no better way than diversifying the portfolio to help you avoid the inevitable peaks of investing.

Why Diversifying the Portfolio a Favorable Act?

Diversification means spreading your investment across multiple portfolios, such as stocks, bonds, real estate, and commodities. This strategy can help minimize risk and increase the likelihood of achieving long-term financial goals. By allocating your investments across different asset classes, you can reduce the impact of market volatility on your portfolio. If one asset class experiences a dip, the other asset classes in your portfolio can help compensate for the potential losses. It is an approach that is specifically designed to reduce the risk in the share market.

Benefits of Portfolio Diversification

Have you ever considered the possibility of losing all your stocks in a market crash? Let's be honest; none of us would ever prepare for any worst-case scenario. We believe it might not happen to us and refuse to consider it. But remember it was the stock market crash that turned out to be the major catalyst behind the Great Depression? Given the history, I have started seeing the process of diversification as the best friend of investors.

Considering the above-mentioned, I have gathered some amazing benefits of diversification so that you can better understand how it works.

1. Different Market and Economic Conditions

A diversified portfolio allows you to take advantage of different economic and market conditions. For instance, when interest rates are low, bonds may not provide as much return on investment, but stocks may perform better. By diversifying your portfolio, you can capture the potential benefits of each asset class and adjust your allocation based on changing market conditions.

2. Managing Risk Factors

Diversification helps to spread the risk across various asset classes and investments, which reduces the overall risk of loss. It further tries to maximize the return over a long duration. Since not all assets behave similarly and tend to have different tenures, they are more likely to maximize the return through diversification.

A diversified portfolio that may include fixed income, real estate, equity, and so on is widely considered an excellent way to earn a greater and long-term return.

3. Managing Your Investment Objective

Diversification is a great way to manage your investment objectives and timeline. If you have a long-term investment horizon, you may want to allocate more of your portfolio to stocks that have previously provided higher returns over the long term. On the other hand, if you have a shorter-term investment goal, you may want to allocate more of your portfolio to bonds or other fixed-income assets, which can provide more stability and predictable returns.

However, your ideal asset allocation depends on your financial goals, risk tolerance, and investment timeline. If you work with a financial expert, you can easily determine the appropriate asset allocation for your specific needs, avoiding most of the stakes.

4. Reduces the Impact of Market Volatility

As mentioned previously, diversification involves spreading your investments across different asset classes, sectors, and geographic locations. By doing so, you can reduce your exposure to market volatility, which is the tendency for prices to fluctuate over short periods of time.

One of the main reasons diversification reduces market volatility is that it helps mitigate the impact of individual events or economic conditions that can affect a particular asset or sector. Suppose you only invest in one type of stock or commodity. In that case, your portfolio will be highly vulnerable to any negative news or developments in the stock market industry or market fluctuation. But if you also invest in other sectors, such as stocks or currency exchange, you can reduce the impact of such events on your overall portfolio.

5. Enhances Portfolio Stability

Given the stock market's unpredictable nature, a strong, diversified portfolio must stand firm against market vulnerability.

These portfolios are less susceptible to sudden changes in the market and provide more stable and predictable returns.

Besides that, diversification is also used to enhance portfolio stability by spreading the risk across multiple investments. This means the portfolio is less vulnerable to the volatility of any asset, sector, or geographic region. As a result, diversification can help to create a more stable portfolio that can compete against the fluctuation of the market.

Diversification enhances portfolio stability by reducing the portfolio's overall risk. When you invest in a single asset, you are exposed to the full risk of that asset. However, by investing in multiple assets, you reduce the portfolio's overall risk.

Mitigating Risk Through Diversification

Every investor wants to generate a competitive return on investment, but their major concern is the risk factor. The real question is how to limit the risk factor in investment.

A good way through which diversification can mitigate risk is by reducing the impact of any single asset or sector on your overall portfolio. By investing in a variety of assets, you spread your risk and avoid the negative impact that any one asset or sector may have on your portfolio. For instance, if you invest only in commodities, you could face significant losses if there is a market crash or downturn.

By diversifying your investments across different sectors, such as the stock market, gold, or mutual funds, you can reduce the impact of any single sector on your overall portfolio.

Furthermore, diversification helps in mitigating risk by smoothing out the returns gradually. It is a given that different asset classes tend to perform differently under different economic conditions. But the point is, if you have a mix of defensive and cyclical sectors in your portfolio, you can reduce the volatility of your returns over time and potentially achieve more stable long-term growth. For instance, defensive sectors like utilities might perform better during a recession than technology and consumer discretionary sectors. Additionally, diversification helps mitigate risk by lowering the correlation between your investments.

Correlation refers to the degree to which two assets move in the same direction. By investing in assets that have low or negative correlations with each other, you can reduce the overall volatility of your portfolio. For instance, stocks and bonds usually have a negative correlation. This means that bonds tend to perform better when stocks are down.

All in all, having both stocks and bonds in your portfolio can reduce the overall volatility of your returns.

Diversification and Risk Assessment

Risk assessment plays a key role in any investment strategy, and diversifying your portfolio is no exception. Diversification involves spreading your investments across asset classes and securities to reduce overall risk. Not to mention, it's equally significant to understand the risks associated with each investment to make informed decisions pertaining to diversification.

An easy way to assess risk when diversifying your portfolio is to consider the historical performance of different asset classes. I am not saying that past performance would guarantee concrete future results; however, it can provide valuable insight into how an asset may perform in different market conditions. For instance, stocks are usually preferred because they provide higher returns over the long term, but it cannot be ignored that they tend to be more volatile than bonds.

Another way to assess risk before you get into diversification is by considering your investment time horizon. Short-term investments typically carry more risk than long-term investments, as they are more susceptible to market fluctuations. If you have a short-term investment horizon, you may want to focus on low-risk investments like bonds and currency. Conversely, if you have a long-term investment horizon, you may want to take on higher-risk investments like stocks, as you have more time to avoid market volatility.

Strategies to Diversify Your Portfolio Effectively

Diversifying your investment could reduce the investment risk while giving you a chance for long-term growth. Having said that, a good portfolio involves investing in various assets to spread risk and improve returns. Here are some of the proven strategies that can help you diversify your portfolio efficiently.

- **Diversifying Across Assets Classes**

One of the most important concepts in investment management is diversifying across asset classes. It involves investing in different types of assets, such as stocks, bonds, real estate, commodities, mutual funds, etc. This is great for reducing the risk in a portfolio.

Each asset class owns specific risk factors and distinct characteristics, and a diversified portfolio can help balance these characteristics and improve overall performance.

Let's quickly dig into why one should diversify across asset classes.

1. The first and foremost reason to diversify across asset classes is to reduce the impact of market volatility on the portfolio.

2. Different asset classes tend to react differently to market fluctuations, and a diversified portfolio can help offset losses in one area with gains in another. For example, during a stock market downturn, bonds may provide a stabilizing force and reduce the overall impact on the portfolio.
3. Another reason to diversify across asset classes is to take advantage of different economic cycles.
4. Each asset class has unique risk and return characteristics, and a diversified portfolio can help balance these characteristics to meet the investor's goals and risk tolerance level.

Diversification across asset classes can also help to manage risk. For example, stocks are generally considered riskier than bonds, but bonds may have lower returns. By combining these asset classes, investors can balance risk and return to meet their investment objectives. In addition, by investing in various assets, investors can reduce the risk of exposure to any asset class or investment.

- **Determining Correlation**

When it comes to portfolio management, it is crucial to consider the correlation between assets because it can significantly impact the portfolio's risk and return rate.

An easy way to determine the correlation between assets is with the help of statistical measures such as the correlation coefficient. The correlation coefficient is a statistical measure that ranges from -1 to +1 and indicates the strength and direction of the relationship between two variables. A positive correlation coefficient indicates a positive relationship, while a negative correlation coefficient indicates a negative relationship. A correlation coefficient of zero indicates no relationship between the two variables.

In portfolio management, it is generally desirable to have assets with low or negative correlation. This is because of the fact that assets tend to move unaccompanied when they are not highly correlated, which can help reduce overall portfolio risk.

- **Diversifying Within the Asset Classes**

Previously, we have seen why diversifying across the asset classes could be a good strategy for investors, but now is the time to uncover what diversification within the asset classes can do. Diversifying within the asset classes includes investing in various securities or instruments within the same asset class, such as different stocks or bonds.

Diversification within asset classes is to invest in securities with different risk and return characteristics. For instance, within the stock market, investors can invest in large-cap and small-cap stocks or stocks of different sectors, such as healthcare or finance. Investing in multiple stocks can potentially reduce the risk of losses in one area with gains in another.

- **Diversify Through Location**

Diversification by location refers to holding securities through multiple regions while restricting the risk factor. How so? Investing in multiple regions can benefit from different economic and market conditions and reduce their exposure to any country or region's economic or political happenings.

You can diversify your portfolio through the location by investing in global or international funds. These funds invest in companies located in different regions around the world.

As an investor, you can also diversify through the location by investing in real estate in different regions. Real estate investments may include physical properties, real estate investment trusts (REITs), or other real estate funds. Investing in real estate in different regions can benefit from the growth and opportunities in different real estate markets.

- **Rebalanced Your Portfolio Regularly**

Remember, regularly rebalancing your investment portfolio is essential to ensure that your asset allocation aligns with your investment goals and risk tolerance.

1. One of the major reasons to rebalance your portfolio regularly is to maintain the appropriate level of risk for your investment goals.
2. The second thing is if you rebalance your portfolio regularly, you will be able to take advantage of market fluctuations.

Undoubtedly, markets can be volatile, and different asset classes can perform differently at different times. By rebalancing, you can sell assets that have performed well and buy assets that have underperformed, buying low and selling high.

- **Consider Your Risk Tolerance Level**

Before you get into investment diversification, it is critical to consider the investor's risk tolerance. Risk tolerance refers to the degree of risk an investor is willing to take in their investments. Different investors have different risk tolerance levels, and it is important to consider this when diversifying strategies.

Investors with a high-risk tolerance may be more willing to invest in riskier assets, such as stocks of startups or emerging companies. They may also be willing to invest in assets with higher volatility, such as commodities or currencies. On the other hand, investors with a low-risk tolerance may prefer safer assets, such as bonds or real estate investment trusts, that offer more stable returns. However, when diversifying investment strategies, it is important to balance the portfolio with different levels of risk.

In conclusion, investment diversification is an important strategy that can help investors minimize risks and increase their chances of long-term success. By investing in multiple assets, investors can spread their risk and reduce the impact of any single investment performance on their overall portfolio. This can help protect investors from sudden market deflation or economic shocks, ensuring their investments remain stable and profitable over the long term.

Key Takeaways from This Chapter:

Chapter 12 discusses the concept of diversification in investment and how it can be beneficial for achieving long-term financial goals. By investing in different asset classes, investors can reduce the impact of market volatility on their portfolios. This approach is designed to reduce the risk in the share market and increase the likelihood of achieving long-term financial goals.

The chapter highlights the benefits of portfolio diversification, including reducing the impact of market volatility on the portfolio and minimizing risk by spreading investments across different asset classes. The chapter also discusses the importance of maintaining a diversified portfolio by regularly rebalancing and adjusting it as market conditions change. Furthermore, the chapter highlights the potential drawbacks of diversification, such as increased complexity and reduced potential returns. However, these risks can be minimized through careful planning and monitoring.

Here are a few of the strategies to diversify the portfolio effectively

- Diversifying within asset classes involves investing in various securities or instruments within the same asset class, such as different stocks or bonds.

- Diversifying through location refers to holding securities through multiple regions while restricting the risk factor.
- Regularly rebalancing your investment portfolio is essential to ensure that your asset allocation aligns with your investment goals and risk tolerance.
- It is critical to consider the investor's risk tolerance before investing in diversification.

Chapter 13: The Success Story of Sadiq Al Mulla

"After all, it's what we've done that makes us what we are."

— Jim Croce

Most people believe that becoming a millionaire is about making a ton of money, but they fail to understand that before you start generating revenue, you need to have a proper mindset that will govern your path accurately.

It is natural for humans to pursue wealth. Besides that, financial independence is a common aspiration for many people. However, realizing this dream at an appropriate time is what makes the difference, which was the case for me as well. My pursuit of a millionaire mindset started during my university years, which became more substantial with my first job as soon as I started working as a salaried employee. The monthly income I received at that time was an incentive for my dream that motivated me to create a crystal-clear plan and pushed me forward to follow short-term, medium-term, and long-term goals.

I was always sure of what I had in mind. My plan was direct, yet it was ambitious. I knew the significance of investing in one's self. I knew the wonders that it could do, and that is what my first step was. I started investing in the power of knowledge. I started a new journey where I learned about finance and entrepreneurship and attended seminars and workshops. I read countless books on wealth creation, not discriminating between good and bad books, because, for me, one thing was clear: every book had something to offer. I started surrounding myself with successful people who always had something to offer, something critical to add to my financial growth.

After seeking knowledge from every nook and corner, it was time to start working on my plan by saving as much money as possible. I focused on setting a goal of saving between 50% and 70% of my monthly income. At that time, it was comparatively more manageable for me since I was unhitched and had no significant responsibilities on my shoulders. I figured it was the best time and opportunity to save more than half of my income. Indeed, keeping a good amount of money aside was a building block to my plan since I needed the capital to invest in generating wealth.

Finally, I started my journey by exploring multiple investment opportunities. In my spare time, I used to rigorously research various investment options, such as stocks, mutual funds, and real estate. With that, I used to weigh the potential risks and rewards attached to investing to ensure that I was making informed decisions that aligned with my goals and risk tolerance.

My journey of investing in the Dubai stock market started in the mid-1980s, which certainly was not as simple as it might appear from a distance. During those times, the option of investing in local shares of Dubai-based companies was highly limited. The investor barely had choices and faced challenges in finding sellers and buyers. It was the time when the investment was made either by purchasing stocks directly from the owner of the shares through personal means and contacts or by searching for classified ads. The investors were supposed to wait for the sellers to contact them and buy the shares directly.

The investors could have opted for a second option by contacting the share departments of public companies and leaving their contact numbers with them. But the real stumbling block in this process was its excessive time consumption. Moreover, their prices were decided based on previously traded prices with almost no bargaining between the sellers and the buyers.

A few years later, some companies took the initiative to open brokerage firms dealing with local shares, which became an alternative source of investment. Therein lies the actual problem. This alternative investment method was extremely costly since buyers and sellers had to pay a 1% brokerage fee. Naturally, it became the least favorable way of investment among the investors of that time.

Finally, the formal stock market in Dubai was established. It was the year 2000 when investors were provided with an authorized platform to trade securities and other financial instruments. The government set the Dubai Financial Market (DFM) on March 26, 2000, intending to provide investors with a platform to trade securities and other financial instruments. This included listing and trading equities, bonds, mutual funds, and other securities. In addition to that, DFM also started offering a range of market data, indices, and other services to investors and market participants. The next big step in developing the UAE financial services sector was the Abu Dhabi Securities Exchange (ADX), formed on November 15, 2000.

A Journey Full of Obstacles

Like any other human, my investment journey was not a piece of cake; instead, it was full of bumps where every challenge was trying to weigh me down. However, I firmly believe facing different challenges means getting an opportunity to learn and grow. Keeping this in mind, I started my investment journey in 1985. Honestly, it was not an ideal time to take a risk since the Iran-Iraq War had impacted the Gulf region badly. The war had left an uncertain and adverse effect on the economy of the Gulf region, precisely on the United Arab Emirates. The fear and dubiousness that were attached to the loss and insolvency left a negative mark on the Middle Eastern investment landscape, increasing the risk factor in all sorts of investments.

A smooth sea never made a skilled sailor. It's the ups and downs that make you a seasoned person. I would say the same in my case. The following events over the course of decades affected my financial journey to becoming a millionaire:

1. The Impact of Operation Desert Storm

It was not before the Iran-Iraq War ceased that the economy started recovering. Given the loss, the process was relatively slow-paced, but at the very least, things were returning to normal until the horrors of the Gulf War in 1990 started lingering, with Iraq invading Kuwait. This historical conflict is generally remembered as Operation Desert Storm or the Gulf War, lasting from January 17, 1991, to February 28, 1991. At first, the stock market witnessed a new low, with the Dow Jones Industrial Average falling by more than 4% on the first day of trading after the invasion. But, over time, the stock market rebounded as the conflict progressed, and the coalition forces achieved quick and decisive victories.

2. Syrian War: An Armed Conflict

Next, it was the year 2011 when the Syrian Civil War began. Ironically, the war started long ago, but nobody knows when it will cease or ever end. The conflict began as a mere protest against the government of President Bashar al-Assad, which took an ugly turn and ended up fueling a war. Since then, it has led to significant human damage. Not to mention, the conflict has also had significant political and economic implications for Syria and the wider region, impacting investors negatively once again.

3. The Ongoing Rivalry of Yemen

In the year 2015, a war broke out in Yemen, which was supported by the alliance of countries led by Saudi Arabia. This gave more than enough reasons to the opposing party to have a military intervention in Yemen. The primary motive behind this conflict was to counter the Houthi rebel group. The ongoing conflict had indirectly affected the country's stock market. The rivalry involved sustained air campaigns, ground fighting, and clashes in Yemen, leaving the economy to decline.

4. The Sudden Outburst of COVID-19

Where the war-like situations between Syria and Yemen left prominent scars on the economic and financial aspects, the COVID-19 pandemic proved to be a disaster for the investment landscape. The stock market and property prices showed an instant price decline and revenue loss due to external variables.

The fall was majorly due to sudden lockdowns and prevailing fears among people. Many firms downsized the companies, leaving people unemployed. Some businesses even closed down as they met huge losses. As a result, many companies went bankrupt, which increased the risk factor connected to investment.

If I talk about myself, investing during these times was indeed challenging. I had to rebalance my investment portfolio according to these economic cycles to minimize negative impacts and manage the risk factors, yet it was worth investing all my time and effort. This difficult journey made me understand the importance of diversification. These various economic cycles taught me several valuable lessons that turn out to be useful even today.

5. Ukraine vs. Russia

In 2022, Ukraine and Russia ended up in a war-like situation. For Ukraine, it was a chaotic time. The political unrest was no joke; on top of that, the sudden conflict backfired and resulted in a bigger loss. The war left a long-lasting shock on the economy, once again leaving investors uncertain. It was the top priority to restore the economy during such crises. This ongoing war has and continues to have a global economic impact on many countries.

During this time, the Ukrainian stock market was key to restoring Ukraine's economy. Many investors took advantage of the low stock prices and invested in the country's stock market, which significantly supported the economy.

The Switch in the Economic Cycle

Since the early years of the 1980s, the global economic cycle has shown significant changes, with far-reaching consequences for businesses, governments, and individuals all over the globe. It is advisable for investors to familiarize themselves with these changes and their implications to make informed decisions about investments, trade, and economic policy.

This period marks one of the essential developments, i.e., the rise of neoliberalism. This political approach favored the importance of free markets, deregulation, and privatization. Their supporters claimed these policies could lead to more remarkable economic growth and efficiency. On the other hand, critics expounded on neoliberal policies and their negative consequences, including discrimination based on status, environmental degradation, and the erosion of worker protections.

Fast forward to the 2000s. It was the decade when economic growth was sustained, especially in emerging markets. However, at the same time, the growth was also marked by significant instability, including the dot-com bubble and the global financial crisis of 2008.

Time passed, and the global economy started to enter a period of slow growth. Governments worldwide implemented low-interest rates and quantitative easing measures to bring about positive economic shifts. As aforementioned, the COVID-19 pandemic has profoundly impacted the global economy in recent years. Governments worldwide implemented lockdowns to slow the spread of the virus, disrupting the economy.

The Rise and Fall of UAE's Economy: An Overview of the Country's Investment Milieu

Since the early years of the 1980s, the UAE has seen a sudden upswing in the economic cycle with persistent setbacks. Not long ago, the UAE became a highly diverse economy, with the government investing heavily in non-oil sectors. But not to forget, this was not always the case. There was a time when the country was highly reliant on its oil export, its only source of revenue.

UAE faced its major economic crisis in the mid-1980s due to the outrageous oil price crash. During those times, the country was entirely relying on oil revenue. The decline in oil prices led to an economic recession, with a high unemployment rate and reduced investment levels.

It was a challenging economic environment for investors with limited opportunities for high investment returns.

The economic situation witnessed sustained economic growth in the 1990s as the government invested a great range of amounts in infrastructure projects, such as the construction of highways, airports, and seaports, facilitating the growth of the tourism and construction sectors. Moreover, this period became a golden time for the real estate market, which boomed with a wave of construction projects driving economic growth.

The UAE continued to experience strong economic growth, driven by high levels of investment in critical sectors. It became a pivot point for the world of finance and banking. The government invested heavily in developing a world-class financial sector, making the UAE home to many large banks, corporations, and institutions.

In the 2000s, the UAE managed to emerge as a crucial financial center, gradually becoming the center for international trade. The government's investment in tourism and real estate finally paid off in economic growth. The country started generating reliable revenue while solidifying its reputation as a tourist destination with iconic landmarks like the Burj Khalifa and the Palm Jumeirah.

The most significant change during this time marks the decision to permit non-citizens to buy and invest in freehold properties in Dubai, followed by Abu Dhabi and other emirates. Now, the investors were presented with an excellent opportunity to invest in real estate as well.

This was an outstanding opportunity for an investor to diversify investment portfolios and gain exposure to the UAE's booming real estate market. Many local and international investors took advantage of this opportunity and invested heavily in properties in the country. The resulting increase in demand for properties helped to drive economic growth and establish the UAE as a major player in the global real estate market.

Moving on to the years 2009 to 2013 where, once again, UAE met some uncertain challenges owing to the global financial crisis in 2008. The country's real estate sector was hit hard during this time, with property prices witnessing a new low. This resulted in putting a hold on many underdeveloped projects. Nonetheless, the government responded quickly to the crisis, implementing various measures to stabilize the economy.

The year 2014 to 2018 was the recovery time for the UAE's economy. At this point, the economy started moving towards stability and growth. The government continued to invest in important sectors such as tourism, technology, and renewable energy; conversely, the real estate sector began to rebound. The UAE also benefited from rising oil prices during this period, which helped them to boost government revenues and support economic growth.

Then, the world was taken over by COVID-19, leaving a negative impact not only on the UAE's economy but also disrupting the global market. UAE faced a decline in oil prices and a sudden drop in tourism revenues, which were the main drivers of the UAE's economy.

Despite the uncertain challenges, the UAE's economy has recovered to a great extent, with an increase in oil prices and the easing of restrictions. The government has committed to diversifying and investing in critical sectors such as technology and tourism, positioning the country for continued growth.

How I Started My Journey in the Stock Market

My journey in the stock world started in the UAE. By then, I had saved up a small amount from my job and wanted to put it to good use by investing in the stock market. My vision was clear; I wanted my savings to grow rather than make it stagnant in one place. My priority was to add more value to what I have saved so far, so I started small, with a few thousand dollars, and gradually built up my portfolio over time. The strategy was to invest my savings from time to time into stocks while diversifying my passive income.

As soon as my portfolio grew, I started diversifying into different industries, such as banking, telecommunications, services, and energy. This helped me to spread my risk and minimize the impact of any one sector on my overall portfolio. I also reinvested the dividends received from my investments to help grow my portfolio even further. Year after year, my portfolio expanded, and I learned more about the stock market and how it worked.

After a while, I moved to the UK and later to the USA, where I continued to invest in the stock market, using the same strategy. I did my research and found that investing in the stock market in these countries was similar to the UAE, but there were some major differences, too, especially in how it was regulated. It took me more than a bit of research and advice from financial advisors to navigate these differences while I continued to grow my portfolio.

Bear in mind even when my strategy was for long-term investments, I did not forget to work on my portfolio. Instead, I managed it regularly, making changes as and when required. My investment portfolio was reclassified in a way that aided me in maximizing the return. This helped me stay ahead of the curve and take advantage of any opportunities.

While I was thriving already, I knew it wasn't the end; it was just the beginning. I knew that I wanted to diversify further by investing in real estate, but real estate investment meant a long-term promise with a significant amount of funds that I lacked at that time. Therefore, I patiently waited until I had built up sufficient net worth through my stock market investments before I decided to take a step into the real estate world.

Continuing to Build on Experience

I have been on a trading journey for quite a long time now. My long haul began when I was still a student who planned to learn and absorb as much as possible. For that, I became more inclined towards self-development activities and building a network that would benefit me. Meanwhile, I devised a clear ten-year plan to achieve my first obstacle of accumulating USD 1 million.

Once my initial goal was achieved, I set my sights on even greater levels of wealth, with subsequent goals of accumulating $5 million and $20 million and eventually continuing the journey in the coming years. I understand it must be hard to believe, but let me be honest. There is no hard and fast rule to it. Anybody can do this as long as they are focused on their goal. Your constant effort can get you there. In addition to that, leaping into your investment journey with stocks is a good pick, but do you know that reinvesting dividends can also help build a sufficient net worth and cash flow? Remember, the moment you accumulate a good amount of capital, you should move to the next step, i.e., diversify your portfolio by investing in real estate.

When it comes to real estate investment, you do not necessarily have to stick to any particular form; instead, it could be done through various forms, including:

- Buying a piece of land and constructing a commercial or residential property;
- Purchasing a ready property from the secondary market;
- Buying a new property from a reputable developer.

However, before investing in real estate, I suggest you wait until you have sufficient capital at your disposal since the investment requires a considerably large amount of money, turning it into a long-term investing plan.

My strategy for real estate investment was more or less the same. Considering the return and growth chances, I found myself more inclined to buy residential property over commercial land. Here's what helped me along the way:

1. Buying residential properties in good locations with potential growth.
2. Investing in new properties from reputed developers with a freehold for all nationalities.
3. A good payment plan and a short delivery time of no more than two years are essential.
4. Mid to high-class properties are also a good investment opportunity as they offer a higher return and growth in value.

This was the strategy that I developed, ensuring my goals and cash flow aligned well. Sometimes, I took loans to bridge the payment gap between my finances and the due date of payments. However, it was a sealed deal never to allow the loan to exceed more than thirty percent of the property's actual value. This was quite an efficient strategy that helped me become what I am today.

Believe it or not, real estate is one of the greatest ways to accumulate wealth, especially for longer terms. Yet, to maximize this investment's benefits, it is necessary to adopt a strategic approach. In my case, I chose to take advantage of payment plan flexibility to accelerate my real estate portfolio.

By leveraging the upcoming cash flow and income, you can make more prominent and frequent real estate investments. This can lead to quicker portfolio growth and higher returns over the long term. Moreover, using rental income to fund continued investments and repay short-term bridge loans, the investor can maintain a steady cash flow stream while minimizing risk.

This brings us to the key advantage of real estate investment: its potential to adjust to inflation. As rental rates increase with time, the investor gets a chance to capture the growth and benefit from higher income. Besides that, with the increase in property values, the investor can build equity in their portfolio, providing a valuable source of long-term wealth.

Investing can seem complicated and intimidating, but it's actually a powerful way to create wealth and improve your financial situation. One of the best investment opportunities lies in the stock market, which has the potential to generate substantial returns over time.

The Sadiq's Guide to Investing

In the contemporary world, where the cost of living continues to rise, and financial markets play an increasingly important role, learning about different investment opportunities has become more critical than ever. With the proper knowledge and strategies, anyone can take advantage of these opportunities to improve their standard of living and achieve their financial goals. To kick start in the financial world effectively, I have gathered some of the effective and practical investing steps that would serve you as a perfect guide.

1. Decide the Kind of World You Want to Make for Yourself

Your first step should be deciding what kind of world you want to create for yourself and your family. This will allow you to develop a successful financial estimate. Sadly, most people don't take the time to consider this factor and usually struggle to achieve their financial goals. Knowing what you want to do with your life is equivalent to developing a vision for your future. This vision will help you make informed decisions that will align with your long-term goals.

The moment you are clear about the vision of your future, you can set your investment goals. It's highly critical to make your goals specific and quantifiable so that you can track your progress over time. For instance, if you aim to save USD 1,000 monthly for twelve months, you can break it down into smaller monthly goals to help you stay on track.

2. Invest in Yourself to Make Your Future Better

Once, a literary artist said, "An investment in self-development pays the highest dividends," and trust me, this adage is one of the most useful things I have come across in my life. Investing in yourself for a better future is the first rule to succeed in any field. This is the most critical step for building a successful and fulfilling life. You can discover new opportunities and maximize your potential in any area of your life through your talents, interests, and skills. Whether through formal education or self-directed learning, developing your knowledge and expertise can help unlock new career opportunities while increasing your earning potential.

3. The Power of Networking

Where education and skill-building act as a foundation upon which you learn to build your future, network building significantly improves your visibility. Associating yourself with a credible network and connecting with others within your industry or field of interest is vital for any investor. By broadening your circle and building relationships with others, you can gain valuable insight and develop a deeper understanding of the financial markets.

4. Multiple Streams of Income

With constant price increases and growing inflation, creating multiple income streams has become all the more necessary. Diversifying income can increase your financial security and build long-term wealth. Remember, the more income you make, the faster you will be able to achieve your dream. Moreover, having more than one source of income is a great way to ensure that you always stay financially covered. Tell me, what could be better than that?

5. Cut the Cost

Keeping a record of your spending and avoiding unnecessary expenses is a must before you get into investing. This is among the most important steps to accumulating wealth. Reducing your living costs and living below your means might not be everybody's preference; however, a little compromise at an initial stage can end up becoming highly remunerative for you. This means keeping a record of your spending habits and finding ways to cut costs wherever possible can be worth your while.

Cutting costs may involve changing your lifestyle, for instance, downsizing to an apartment from a house or car, not visiting cafés frequently, or, at times, it could mean shopping smart from year-end sales. By keeping your expenses as low as possible, you can free up more of your income to invest in your future and build long-term wealth.

Creating a personal budget is an important step in achieving financial security and building wealth, especially if you're in your twenties. By developing a budget, you can effectively manage your income and expenses, identify areas where you can cut back on spending, and allocate funds towards saving and investing for the future.

6. Creating an Effective Budget

It is safe to say that your budget plays a vital role in leading a path toward your financial success. It is an efficient way to outline your expenses, which can help you to live within your means. Not to mention, a well-developed budget can help you sustain financial stability as well; however, budget deficits can lead to borrowing and high interest rates. That is why budgeting is an essential part of saving. Living beyond your means can quickly throw you into debt, leading to financial instability and hindering your ability to accumulate wealth.

Here's how you can quickly get into budgeting. As a starter, assess your income and expenses carefully. Explore your monthly take-home pay and then jot down your monthly fixed expenses. Once you determine your income and expenses, you can easily find areas to cut back on spending, such as dining out or buying things that are not required.

This is how you can efficiently allocate a portion of your income toward building wealth. The key is to prioritize your expenses and set realistic goals to avoid being demotivated. *A small tip:* Set aside funds for unexpected situations so that your progress doesn't get knocked down in the face of an emergency.

7. Add Money to Your Saving Pot

As I have always said, saving money is significant in building wealth; the earlier you start, the better returns you will be rewarded with. One of the excellent ways to strengthen your financial journey is by initially saving approximately between 20% and 70% of your income. The savings can vary from person to person, depending on each person's circumstances. Here, you need to remember that the ability to put money aside to save it is a rich mindset you must adopt. Once you have decided to become a millionaire, it should be your prime goal to save most of what you have earned, and then your second step should be investing.

It takes one quick search on Google to find multiple ways to save money; however, my approach to savings is slightly different. I don't prefer adding only the leftover amount to my savings account; instead, I ensure to go the extra mile and extract every penny from the expenses that can be cut off easily. That is how I have saved and accumulated this much wealth.

My strategic plan for saving includes the following:

- Paying off credit card bills in full to avoid high-interest charges will help you eliminate debt. If you know how much interest you are paying to the bank on your debts, you will think more toward paying it off as soon as possible and keeping your money in a savings account to receive interest/profit.

- Buying things during regular sales, buying necessary food commodities at wholesale prices, especially the ones with long-expiry date products (rice, sugar, wheat, etc.).

- Setting saving goals and a timeline to make saving easier. For example: You need to buy a car with a 10% or 20% down payment or payment in full. Now you have a target and are aware of what you need to save every month in order to achieve your goal.

- Setting up a standing instruction on your bank account to transfer a specific percentage of your salary to a savings account. The amount could be 10%, 20%, 30%, or more monthly.

This might sound absurd at first, but hear me out. If you are a chain smoker, quit smoking right away. Smoking is a luxury that you can't afford at the moment. Quitting smoking means you will be saving about USD 3,000 to 5,000 yearly. Additionally, start taking a staycation instead of spending all your money on overseas holidays and expensive airline tickets. Look for cheap tickets, package travel, off-season travel, travel groups, etc. This will save you at least 50% of the normal cost.

Other ways may include:

- Saving on utility costs at home by installing solar panels to cut back on electricity bills.
- Packing your lunch/dinner instead of buying it at work. Buying lunch or dinner will cost you $10, but bringing lunch or dinner from home will cost you only $3. This way, you can save $2,400, which will help you in generating additional income.
- Avoiding costly cellphone data plans. Subscribe to a plan that meets your actual requirements. That will save you unnecessary expenses, and you can save up to $500 a year.
- Skipping the morning coffee. You can make your own coffee as well as your breakfast and have your coffee in a flask that will stay warm for twelve hours. This will save you $10 every day. Over the course of a year, you can save $3,000.
- Cutting back on rent by living with a roommate or

downsizing to a smaller apartment. At this point, avoiding rent should be your priority. Try purchasing your own house or apartment through a down payment and a long-term mortgage loan. Don't fear the idea of taking out a loan. This property is an asset that will benefit you in the future.

8. Create Passive Income

With passive income, you no longer depend on one income source for your living expenses. However, starting passive income streams without any prior experience may be daunting, but it is completely possible with a little research and effort. The best way to get started with your passive income is by investing in dividend stocks. Dividend stocks provide investors with regular income payments without requiring active involvement. Researching and investing in dividend stocks with a track record of consistent payouts can be a relatively low-risk way to generate passive income. With that, renting out your property or a spare room like Airbnb can help you generate a steady stream of passive income. Besides that, you can diversify your passive income by investing in different assets, ultimately increasing your earning potential.

9. Develop a Millionaire Mindset

To become a millionaire, you must believe that you have what it takes to be a millionaire; you should possess a millionaire mindset. Not many people will tell you, but having a millionaire mindset is a must-have approach to achieving financial success. You need to have a positive attitude and disciplined approach toward financial planning. Committing to a financial plan and setting short, medium, and long-term goals is essential. Yet, there are certain things that should be taken into account before you set any goal. Most importantly, consider the kind of life you want. This is an important part since it will determine your goal. Money plays a crucial role in achieving life goals; hence, a well-thought-out financial plan is crucial.

Having short-term financial goals, including saving money and keeping it in a savings account, can help you earn profit. Learning about investment and stock markets is also necessary to make informed decisions at this stage. Once sufficient funds are saved, one can start investing in selected stocks.

Medium-term goals, ranging from one to ten years, require careful cash flow management to pay for expenses like higher education, a house, or mortgage payments. Saving, investing, and liquidating funds are necessary to achieve these goals.

If your goal is long-term, spanning over ten years, it requires breaking down the goal into smaller milestones that can be achieved with regular investment and appreciation. Suppose that your goal is to accumulate $1 million in ten years; now, you are required to plan, save, and invest a certain amount monthly. *A quick tip:* Reinvestment of dividends can accelerate the growth of your portfolio rather quickly. It is essential to revisit long-term goals every five years to ensure you are on track to achieve them.

Additionally, starting investing from an early age with a diversified portfolio is essential. Invest in stocks for at least ten years or until you reach a specific financial goal. Once achieved, gradually diversify into real estate while investing in stocks with a 70/30 split. Rebalancing your portfolio throughout your investment plan is crucial for optimal results.

10. Get Started with Your Venture

Creating a successful venture is not something one can do overnight. Building a business from scratch that will last long is nothing like making a few dimes. It requires time, patience, and constant learning about new trends. However, it is an excellent way to accumulate wealth. It permits you to earn additional income and build assets that can appreciate in value over time. It is highly beneficial, especially when you have started early, which gives your business significant time to grow.

Additionally, you can leverage your existing network and skillset to establish a successful business in no time. As a full-timer, you can use your remaining free time to work on your business and build it up gradually. This can help you create a substantial source of passive income in the future and potentially even achieve financial independence.

11. Implementation of Leverage

It might come to you as a surprise, but debt does not necessarily have to be bad. It could sometimes act as a valuable tool, depending on its use. However, understanding the distinction between good and bad debt is what makes the difference. Good debt usually includes a home loan. This can help you save money on rent and add assets that can appreciate and grow your wealth over time. Here, a mortgage can be taken as an example of good debt because it helps you build equity in a home, which can increase in value over time, providing a source of wealth that you can tap into later on. This is similar to the case of taking out a student loan, which is an investment in education that can help you increase your earning potential and improve your job prospects in the future.

On the contrary, borrowing money with no plan to invest or seek profit is regarded as bad debt and should be avoided at any cost. Moreover, if you borrowed money to purchase assets, but the asset decreased in value over time, it is also considered bad debt. A very common example of bad debt is credit card debt because it often comes with high interest rates, and you can quickly lose the record of your spending.

As we proceed to the end of this book, I hope you have acquired a deeper understanding of managing your personal finances and are now equipped with the strategies and tools necessary to take control of your financial future.

Let's be honest... Managing money is a lifelong journey where you will encounter hundreds of peaks and valleys along the way. Nonetheless, implementing the principles and strategies outlined in this book can make your life much easier, allowing you to navigate the financial landscape and mitigate the risk without much hassle.

Always remember, financial success is not about having the most money or the fanciest possessions. It is about living a life that offers you purpose, security, and contentment.

Key Takeaways from This Chapter:

The concluding chapter talks about the author's personal journey as he talked about the time when he started having a millionaire mindset, i.e., during his university years, but it became more substantial once he started working as a salaried employee. The author understood the importance of investing in oneself and began a new journey of finance and entrepreneurship by attending seminars and workshops. Saving money was a critical building block in the author's plan, and they set a goal of saving between 50% and 70% of their monthly income. They then started exploring multiple investment opportunities in stocks, mutual funds, and real estate and researched potential risks and rewards to ensure informed decision-making.

In addition to that, the author discusses his journey in the stock market and how it started in the UAE with a small amount of savings that they wanted to grow. They used a strategy of investing their savings into stocks from time to time while diversifying their passive income. As their portfolio grew, they diversified into different industries to spread their risk and reinvested their dividends to help grow their portfolio further.

In addition to that, the concluding chapter consists of Sadiq's guide – six effective and practical investing steps.

- Setting specific and quantifiable investment goals is crucial to track your progress over time.
- The second step is to invest in yourself for a better future.
- Associating yourself with a credible network and connecting with others within your industry or field of interest is vital for any investor.
- Creating multiple streams of income which can increase financial security and build long-term wealth.
- Cutting costs is the fifth step to accumulating wealth, as it involves keeping a record of spending habits and finding ways to cut costs wherever possible.
- Creating an effective budget which plays a vital role in leading a path toward financial success.

Overall, the concluding chapter is about the author's successful journey in the stock market and real estate investment due to his clear vision, strategy, patience, and willingness to learn and adapt.

Made in the USA
Columbia, SC
13 February 2024

7aaa303b-2e9b-4c32-b843-79d7587a9128R01